Thinking Aloud

Fragments of Autobiography

Peter Cotes

THINKING ALOUD

Fragments of Autobiography

PETER OWEN · London

In memory of

JM

She's stuck to me through thick and thin
When luck was out, when luck was in
Oh what a pal to me she's bin
My Dear Old Girl

With acknowledgements to *My Old Dutch*
(Albert Chevalier)

PETER OWEN PUBLISHERS
73 Kenway Road London SW5 0RE

First published in Great Britain 1993
© Peter Cotes 1993

A catalogue record for this book is available
from the British Library

ISBN 0–7206–0900–3

Printed and bound in Great Britain

Contents

Illustrations

(on pages 75 to 82)

'The Guv'nor' in Napoleonic stance
Our mother as a girl
The author impersonating Vesta Tilley
The four Boulting boys with 'Nannie'
The Boulting family at home in Hove
Marriage!
Donald Wolfit and Rosalind Iden in *The Master Builder*
Joan Miller and Wilfrid Lawson in *The Wooden Dish*
Programme from the first night of *that* play
Joan Miller in Anouilh's *Medea*
Joan Miller and Alec Clunes in *Julius Caesar*
Julie Andrews and Andrew Cruickshank in *Mountain Fire*
Flora Robson, Joan Miller and Joyce Carey in
The Old Ladies
Joan Miller as Queen Constance in *King John*
Joan Miller and Roger Moore in *A Pin to See the Peepshow*
'A great, if harrowing, performance . . . in *A Pin to See the Peepshow*'
Partners in and out of the theatre
Joan, as she was for so long

ACT ONE

Prologue
Yesterday and Today
Pictures in the Fire
Going to the 'Fumes'
Brothers and Others
Professionalism in Play Production
Telly-Ho!
No Run
Short Run
Long Run

Author's Note

Apologies, despite the tiresome mod habit 'never complain, never explain', to those who expect chronological order.

This is not only a narrative, but a bit of an anthology containing selected hand-picked 'moments' – those less interesting I may have skipped, but I have not fibbed. I have sometimes omitted when I thought that the truth might hurt good people still living – and the memories of others now in the past.

PC

Acknowledgements

In writing this book I have made use of an accumulation of press cuttings, a mound of correspondence and boxes full of old theatre programmes and variety and cabaret date books; I have also made use of the writings of others, always acknowledging my sources wherever possible. Some few of the editors and publishers are beyond the reach of my thanks; to the survivors – Diana Bishop, Peter Black, Kenneth Hurren, John Knight, Ronald Harwood, Eric Shorter, Bobby Robi, Louise Wright, Barbara Toy and Cecil Wilson – my thanks are due.

I would also like to thank: Moira Johnston, Ludovic Kennedy, Nesta Pain and my agent Jeffrey Simmons, for reading the script in its early stages and encouraging me to continue; Louis Mahony, for reading several of Joan's poems against apartheid, being one of its victims; Gwen Robyns; Jill Foulston and Juliet Standing of Peter Owen Publishers; Jane Russ, who typed the MS many times on her word-processor, proving herself a constant 'doer' and a tireless worker throughout 'operations' (in more senses of the word than one). Doctors Bob Cooper and David Edwards are owed a special word of gratitude, as are such fighters against injustices as C.H. Rolph, Benedict Birnberg and (again) Ludovic Kennedy.

PC

Prologue

You have to begin to lose your memory, if only in bits and pieces, to realise that memory is what makes our lives. Life without memory is no life at all. . . . Our memory is our coherence, our reason, our feeling, even our action. Without it, we are nothing. . . .

Luis Buñuel

I have a personal file labelled 'Career' into which I have put, over the years, miscellaneous letters and papers on this and that subject which appeared to be of interest at the time. Now that my career is not quite past, what should one do with such an accumulation of documents, press books, photographs, jottings and all the rest of the documentation that indicates a busy, varied and occasionally exciting life?

These miscellanea are, of course, still of some nostalgic value to me, but will they inform and, more important still, entertain others? They are, in their present disconnected form, of little interest. Yet perhaps each one might form some sort of thread through a story that could prove of interest to theatre folk, theatre-goers and later generations. The greater part of my career belongs to a bygone age that will never recur (this in itself might be of interest to theatrical historians); it was spent in the service of the theatre. In my heyday the West End and Broadway were still the centres of world entertainment and before then, C.B. Cochran dubbed the London Pavilion 'The Centre of The World'. Great Britain with its record of theatrical accomplishment still held more responsibility for advancing the living stage than any other country in the world.

It may be worthwhile then, to try to recall a few of those bits and pieces of that career while the memories are undimmed and my personal archives can still jog my memory. In doing so I have sought to exclude certain matters which were recalled in a previous autobiography.

As a boy at three different prep schools – Hove, Woodford Green, Taplow – and later at the Italia Conti Stage School, I had always wished to go on the stage professionally. The period between the two great wars was the one in which I grew up, and in which I served an apprenticeship that lasted nearly a score of years. I was a boy actor, stage-manager, and finally the director and producer of plays; I also owned several small theatres at various times in London and the provinces. My first book, *No Star Nonsense* (1949), attempted to set forth my ideas in as practical a fashion as I knew how. It was later to be described by Ivor Brown, editor and drama critic of *The Observer* as 'a challenging declaration of faith in the essentials of tomorrow's theatre'.

At one juncture in my career I was known chiefly as an 'actors' director'. My reputation was based largely on stage, film and television work with actors who became known for the quality of their performances. This possibly placed me in a category apart from the crop of mainstream producers and directors (especially in film and television) who would frequently appear to be absorbed with the decor, costumes and camera angles, at the expense of acting. Such necessary accessories all help to 'stage' rather than direct a play. In the final analysis, its actors and its playwright are what the production must rely upon. I laid out such views, as I saw them 40 years ago, in an Introduction to *No Star Nonsense*, my earlier book. I have since found my main conclusions little changed. Here and there, I would wish to modify what seemed at the time to be firmly held convictions. But only here and there, and not often. Much has happened, though, since the writing of that first book. This book is not intended to be a re-run of my life since that first attempt at fragmentary autobiography. No old scores are settled; revelations there may be, but only for the sake of the record and theatrical history.

Yesterday and Today

Biography is all about cutting – Alan Bennett
And so is Autobiography – Peter Cotes

Unlike a Terry, a Forbes-Robertson, or a Lupino child, I cannot claim to have been destined for the stage as far back as my cradle years, but it was not long before I gained a taste for the theatre which remained for many years a ruling interest in life. I became a regular theatre-goer at the age of four, which was the year when I made my first appearance on the stage, being handed over the footlights at the Portsmouth Hippodrome in order to present a bouquet to the great Vesta Tilley. That queen of male impersonators kissed me in front of the audience and invited me to tea at her hotel. On many future occasions I had the great fun of visiting her at her house on the Fisheries Estate at Maidenhead.

Both my parents had an intense love of the theatre; in his youth my father had toured his own company in South Africa, playing Barry in *A Country Girl* and Dick Phenyl in *Sweet Lavender*, as well as Anthony Absolute and Fagg in *The Rivals*. My father was a wonderful impersonator. I particularly enjoyed it when he sang catchy songs on a cheerful note, 'When Father Laid the Carpet on the Stairs' being one of my favourites. They were the treat of my little life in the days before I actually went to a theatre. And to watch my mother executing a barn dance was an invigorating spectacle. At the time we lived in Southsea, where Albert Chevalier of *My Old Dutch* fame, was an occasional visitor to our house.

My parents went to the theatre at least once a week in Portsmouth, when they attended the variety house, the Hippodrome and sometimes twice a week when they also attended the King's Theatre in Southsea. Soon after my fourth birthday they began to take me with them. I was so completely captivated by the glittering magic that I sat transfixed in my seat, terrified lest I might miss something happening on the stage, where the most interesting people that I had ever seen were drenched in floods of

11

coloured light. The theatre-going experiment was a success, and it became the thing for me to sit between my parents each time they went, after my three brothers (two of whom became known as the Boulting Brothers, the 'British Film Twins') had been tucked up in bed. After all, being twelve months my juniors, they were considered babies! Guy, my youngest brother, was to die at the age of eight-and-a-half of meningitis – a shattering blow at that time, especially to my mother. I should explain that my real name is Boulting. My theatrical pseudonym of Peter Cotes is derived from a house in which we once lived called 'Northcotes'.

I suppose I inherited something of my father's gift for mimicry. Even at that tender age, I followed in his footsteps, like Vesta Tilley in her song, 'Following My Dear Old Dad', and used to come home and sing the songs which had set me 'all of a tingle' at the music hall. I also enjoyed standing in front of a mirror conducting an imaginary band. We soon moved to Hove where the theatre-going was invariably twice weekly, to the Brighton Theatre Royal on Thursday and the Hippodrome on Friday. Marie Lloyd, Vesta Tilley and Albert Chevalier were particular favourites; while later on, Randolph Sutton ('Mother Kelly'), Julian Rose ('Our Hebrew Friend'), Talbot O'Farrell (the Irish Singing Star), and Will Fyffe ('I belong to Glasgow'), were good 'also rans'.

I had a retentive memory and delighted our small family circle in the drawing-room by re-creating what I had seen in the theatre. The straight stage was not neglected, one of my party-pieces being an impression of Eille Norwood as Sherlock Holmes, complete with pipe. My brothers, John and Roy, played Professor Moriarty and Dr Watson, respectively. The war hospitals were crowded with wounded from the battlefields of France, and kind ladies on various committees did all they could to arrange entertainment for the 'dear boys'. My 'act' was considered just the thing, so the poor soldiers had to endure seeing my minute figure dressed in khaki (to represent Vesta Tilley), singing:

> *When the flappers go by,*
> *I'll give each the glad eye,*
> *For one fortnight in July.*

I must admit that the 'boys' were very kind and gave me a rousing reception each time I was inflicted upon them. On these occasions my mother always accompanied me on the piano, and then as for many years later, remained in the background as I took my 'call' at the end of the act. She it was to whom her children owe so much.

My hospital fame spread to such an extent that I found myself invited to Lady Wyndham's York Terrace drawing-room on Sunday afternoons. The widow of the distinguished actor-manager, herself a one-time actress known as Mary Moore, devoted a great deal of time and energy to arranging entertainment for the sick and wounded, and I became a regular 'novelty turn' in the charity concerts she organized. While children of my own age were at kindergarten schools I was hob-nobbing, in my vivid imagination, with Lilian Braithwaite, Marie Tempest and Owen Nares under Lady Wyndham's roof!

Much later I was to become associated with Lady Wyndham's son and grandson, Bronson Albery and Donald Albery, respectively, in such theatrical productions as *The Ugly Duchess* at the Arts, when I was an actor (playing a page-boy), and some thirty years on when I directed *Hot Summer Night* at the New Theatre (now known as the Albery Theatre) in the West End. Later still, I directed an all-black cast in *Janie Jackson*.

A career of some kind seemed to be looming up for me. People who visited our house at Maidenhead eulogized (with drink?), and said something ought to be done about my talent! Belle Reynolds, a neighbour, was a friend of my grandfather, who also lived at Maidenhead. She was a popular pantomime principal boy on tour in her time, but will be best remembered as the wife of Robert Hale (the Drury Lane comedian) and the mother of the popular Binnie and Sonnie Hale, of musical comedy and revue fame. She suggested that the 'infant prodigy' should be trained. In those days, that meant sending a child to Italia Conti. So I was admitted to the establishment that had schooled, amongst others, both Noël Coward and Gertrude Lawrence.

It was not a vintage year. The only one of my contemporaries to make anything like a significant mark in the theatre was Jack Hawkins, although both Walter Gore and Harold Turner went on to make their mark as ballet dancers. We enjoyed ourselves, but wasted far too much time. I suppose it was not completely lost, as it impressed upon me the fact that I was going to make some sort of place for myself in the theatre. Then I imagined that one day I should become a great actor. 'Make-believe' appealed to the child in me far more than simply being myself. I always enjoyed making people believe that I was someone else. I hated the 'boy' parts I played at Conti's, where I was not really happy until I persuaded Bianca Murray, Miss Conti's sister and head drama teacher, into casting me for the part of The Colonel in *Journey's End*, by R.C. Sherriff. I had been taken to see the first production of that record-breaking First World War play with a crowd of students. We witnessed its effect on the audience from seats high in the gallery at the old Prince of Wales Theatre.* I played the part with silvered hair and only a suggestion of a moustache. I was anxious to give the impression of a middle-aged soldier without obscuring my features with all the aids of the make-up box.

An all-star charity matinée at Drury Lane gave me my first chance to make an appearance before a West End audience. It was an auspicious occasion, with King George V and Queen Mary in the Royal Box. Robert Loraine, a popular hero in those days, was playing a scene from *Henry V* with Yvonne Arnaud. As Colonel Robert Loraine he had won the VC in the First World War and was a notable actor of the twenties. I was deputed to carry King Henry's heavy train. Loraine looked at me when I was 'presented' to him in his dressing room, a few minutes before I was to make my London début (not in a *hospital* this time) on the stage of a real theatre: the very stage upon which Edmund Kean had made his name. 'You look too weak to carry this heavy train!' he said. 'We want a sturdier boy.' By then it was too late to do anything about it, so I bore the train and arranged it in a decorative semi-circle about the throne the star actor sat down. I am ashamed to say that in my excitement I tripped over the ermine trimmings and struck a somewhat undignified attitude before my first London public.

A few weeks later I was invited to play a boy's part in the

---

*It was on the same site that a new Prince of Wales Theatre was built, where I was to direct *Pick-Up Girl* nearly a score of years later.

Stage Society production of Eugene O'Neill's *The Great God Brown* at the Strand Theatre. Mary Clare, Moyna Macgill and Hugh Williams (I was to direct Hugh Williams many years later in the successful comedy, *Book of the Month*, at the Cambridge Theatre) are names I remember in the cast and, playing what I think was one of his first good parts in London, was a young actor named John Gielgud.

And shortly after that, again as a boy actor, came a serving-lad role in *The Ugly Duchess*, already mentioned earlier. In the production, directed by the notable Irish actor, W.G. Fay, I played one of my first speaking roles in London opposite a serving wench played by the pretty young actress, Marie Seton. (She later became known as the distinguished film and stage biographer of, amongst others, Sergei Eisenstein, the Russian film maker.) Others I can remember from that cast were such redoubtable 'costume' actors of the day as A.E. Holloway, Eugene Leahy, and William Hartnell, who was largely a comic actor in his later career and was, I seem to recall, the first Dr Who on television.

Esmé Beringer played the title role in this adaptation for the stage by her sister, Vera Beringer, of Lion Feuchtwanger's classic novel. This was a 1930s production at The Arts Theatre Club.* Esmé was a dramatic actress who had once played *Hamlet* in London after Bernhardt had essayed the role in Paris. Her elaborate make-up of the world's ugliest woman took five hours to put on, necessitating her being in her dressing room by 3.00 each afternoon to build herself into a look-alike of de Matzy's celebrated portrait of the Duchess Margarete, the Ugly Duchess, before she was ready to perform.

Bronson Albery, to whom I had been introduced by his mother, Lady Wyndham, was running the Arts in those first years of its existence, and he decided not to continue with the play's run elsewhere, although he owned a number of West End theatres where it might have transferred.

Had I realized in those early years how much an actor's life

---

*Nearly forty years on I was able to offer Esmé Beringer, then eighty, a part in my 1950s production, *Mountain Fire*.

depended upon luck, and the right chance to meet the right people at the right time, I might not have been so keen to become a member of an already overcrowded profession. Only by hard experience was I to discover that so much more than outstanding talent is required in order to gain a place in the theatrical sun.

However, I think I should follow the same course if I had my time over again, as long as I could be sure of discovering a theatre where it was possible to gain complete artistic satisfaction without all the ballyhoo of TV names in electric lights. To my mind, the existence of such a theatre is the one solution for those artists who have become actors and who hope to attain lasting happiness in their work.

Working in the theatre has always been something of an exciting adventure. To me, life without the theatre would be unthinkable. I am still, after all these years, occasionally fascinated by its momentous sense of possibility.

The theatre is still, potentially, teeming with life. Let there be no doubt about that. In my own lifetime it has had to face the onslaught of some fierce rivals. First came moving pictures, which threatened to annihilate 'flesh-and-blood' entertainment. Those celluloid strips captured the thrill of forest fires and alpine avalanches, as well as the comic genius of Charlie Chaplin – but still the playhouse continued to attract sufficient patrons to pay its way. And when sound was added to the moving image, Al Jolson singing 'Sonny Boy' on the screen of every cinema in the country did not completely prevent patrons flocking to old familiar variety theatres for some time afterwards.

Early radio sets seemed to suggest that people would be content with entertainment on their own hearth and never leave home in the evening. But once the novelty wore off, the nine days' wonder became as commonplace as electric light and the washing machine, and took its place in the everyday scheme of things. People continued to be attracted by the magnetism of the playhouse and still enjoyed getting away from their own four walls now and again. As with radio before it, so with its successor television; 'live theatre will die' we were assured. This has not happened. Television has, of course, become a firm favourite with the masses, and only occasionally do such outstanding plays as *Oranges Are Not the Only Fruit*, *The Singing Detective*, and almost everything that Alan Bennett writes for it, represent television drama at its best. Doom was yet again spelt out with the arrival of the video machine on the private market. Large numbers of people bought them, and we were told that 'cinema and the theatre will be dead within a year'. It would seem to be that the exact opposite is the case. Video companies are financing films and, amazingly, going 'out' to the cinema is still popular, as the proliferation of multi-screen cinemas testifies. Meanwhile, theatre still occasionally continues to enchant.

Some newspapers are responsible for spreading far too much pessimism about the theatre. Cecil Wilson, an enthusiast who was journalist, drama critic, entertainments editor and film critic in turn for over forty years on the *Daily Mail* was a notable exception, in appearing to *love* much that he saw! Certain journalists, 'entertainment editors', delight in giving millions of readers the impression that theatre is already dead, except for the large scale musicals such as *Starlight Express*, *Les Misérables*, *The Phantom of the Opera* and *Cats*. If an ill-fated play is withdrawn from the West End after a run of only a week or two it's a 'story' to print, in order to gloat over the theatre's failure to pull in the public. Figures are quoted about the amount of money lost by backers, and news editors indulge themselves at the expense of the poor wretched playwright. The peccadillos of certain actors are all too often blazoned in tabloids' double-banner headlines, and even thoughtful readers led to believe that creative artists are incapable of knowing, in the words of Arnold Bennett, 'what the public wants'.

Neither a television-minded press (both soaps- and series-conscious), nor devastating wars, terrorism, earthquakes and recessions can kill the theatre overnight. As a means of mental stimulation, as well as escapism, it has flourished throughout two world wars. The Kaiser's war brought forth *Chu Chin Chow*. Hitler's war gave us Shakespeare with Wolfit and Olivier at the Old Vic in addition to Fonteyn in *Swan Lake*. Some of the most memorable serious productions of the forties were staged in London during the Second World War: *The Star Turns Red* and *Mourning Becomes Electra* amongst plays, and Olivier's *Long Day's Journey into Night*, Wolfit's *King Lear*, Joan Miller's *Rosmersholm* and Catherine Lacey's *Jane Clegg* amongst performances. Such pieces went to show that servicemen on leave and blitz-weary civilians did not invariably turn to non-stop nudes and sex shops for relaxation.

There must be something in an institution that can survive modern technology and its misuse, as well as constant attack by bombers, massacres abroad, world slumps, recessions, inflation, repossessions and all the rest. Quite obviously it is loved by a large number of the public. Drama, comedy and tragedy in the theatre must be specially designed to suit the times in which we happen to be living. *True* theatre for the nineties.

I have been studying audience reaction ever since my tour of the coalfields in the autumn of 1947. I took a company of players sponsored by the Arts Council and Miners' Welfare Commission to the South Wales mining valley. It proved a revelation. We played *An Inspector Calls* and *Anna Christie*. Our reception was overwhelming, and from the beginning we realized that this specialized public was impressed by the play as much as by the players. There was no blind hero-worship and stupid fan hysteria as far as the cast was concerned. We were without telly names in those days. People came to see 'the drama', as they called it. The work of Priestley and O'Neill obviously meant more to them than the individuals who brought it to life, on the stages of their clubs, institutes and town halls. I suppose with the strong musical heritage in the valleys, it was to be expected that they would be an enthusiastic audience. Louise Hampton told stories of playing Paula Tanqueray in the Rhondda before the First World War, when the curtain rang up at eleven in the morning, so that the men working on the night shift could see the show. Sybil Thorndike played Lady Macbeth and Medea.

Apart from a few isolated instances the miners have not been well served theatrically. They have had to rely on their own amateur theatre, or be content with faintly titillating plays, which aimed at filling houses by appealing always to the trivial side of human nature (I would guess not much appreciated by the Chapel elders). The tours mentioned proved indisputably that if thoughtful entertainment is taken to theatreless industrial areas, it is welcomed in no half-hearted manner. Arthur Miller, Alan Bennett, Hare, Pinter, and Osborne are among the modern writers who sometimes meet the same reception of enthusiasm today as Robertson and Pinero did in their day.

The theatre should not so often be a stomping ground for popular personalities from television who are hyped as actors and actresses. It should surely be a place where actors *and* playwrights are both paramount. Many of the present-day commercial managements are far more interested in vehicles for TV 'names' than in plays of ideas. Dross is sometimes staged because it affords the public a good chance of seeing live some popular star of a TV series, who may not even know how to walk across a stage. Audiences may really go to satisfy their curiosity. But do they imagine they are seeing real acting? Do we devalue the currency by using it in a base way?

This pandering to the lowest common denominator should be combated by well-staged, unselfconscious works of quality, if straight theatre is to flourish as an institution and bear fruit in the future, as it has done in the past. The playwright, through actor and director, must be recognized as the *first* creator; his work brought to life by a group of actors under the guidance of a director who interprets the script as a conductor interprets the score of a composer. The actor should serve the play, *not* the other way around. The director, the actors, the designer, all should see themselves as serving the playwright. For ultimately, it remains true that 'the play's the thing'.

Such was my belief in 1946, when I directed *Pick-Up Girl*. It was sensationally successful, and transferred from our tiny theatre in Notting Hill to the West End. It was gratifying to see a smash hit in the heart of London with a team of actors, all of them good, some of them outstanding, but each willing to be a cog in the wheel, none of them playing for self. This group-theatre method can be very successful. By remaining within the framework and never getting outside the picture, the cast realize that general performances are so much better than if any one player has attempted to obtrude at the expense of the rest. The theatre is the most perishable and yet the most living of all art forms. With every performance it is born anew; with every performance it dies again. The innermost flavour of so personal a place as the playhouse cannot be sufficiently conveyed in print. The director has to elicit that sense of excitement which galvanizes the author's work into life, and to create in the atmosphere that curious sense of vitality, that manifestation for which there is no substitute.

I wrote in *No Star Nonsense*, 'Let us indeed do it as well as we can. It is not a task beyond us'. Those who love the theatre are willing to make any sacrifice. However, it will necessitate servants of the theatre taking stock of themselves to be certain that their love is greater than their desire to be merely personalities on the telly, striving for personal fame and a big bank balance. Writers, directors and actors on whom the theatre of tomorrow depends are often nomads. In the last forty years, although repertory theatre has all but died, some excellent as well as meretricious productions tour the country, and even occasionally manage to get into the West End, such is their 'street success'. There are a few small companies proving that good quality ensemble work continues to be popular. The Edinburgh Fringe spasmodically spawns certain groups who now tour nationally, but the once high standard Liverpool Playhouse is not the haven of culture we once applauded.

As well as my views on the theatre, this book concerns landmarks in my life. Meeting the extraordinary Wilfrid Lawson, today scarcely remembered except by those old enough to have known him, was one such landmark. Being 'drunk as a lord' by 11 o'clock most mornings curtailed Lawson's life, but never interfered with his talent. A great actor, an impossible man. Before I directed him, we were fellow actors and went on tours, and I dressed with him. He had terrible epileptic fits; on trains, in digs, on film sets. I always wondered whether it was the epilepsy that came first or the drinking bouts that preceded his attacks; one did not help the other, and certainly he was a bad bet to raise insurance on!

There was a time in 1955 when, with a career behind me, I had to consider very carefully what I was going to do. Was I going to continue in television after I had been appointed Deputy Head of Drama for the first ITV contractors, Associated Rediffusion? I was already a senior drama director there. I had directed a number of famous film plays that were televised at Shepperton Studios. One of these was St John Ervine's *Jane Clegg*; others, *The Young and The Guilty* and *Woman in a Dressing Gown* were bought for the big screen the day after being transmitted. The whole television cast (with two exceptions) transferred with it. (The part of The Girl in *The Young and The Guilty* was played by Janet Munro in the film version, her first big 'break'.) This was an award winning little film that the critics enthused over. Another later film I started for the Rank organization was *Bitter Harvest* an adaptation of Patrick Hamilton's *Twenty Thousand Streets Under the Sky*. It was not a happy experience in the preliminary stages, and as a film was poorly adapted from Hamilton's fine novel. It was eventually made without me. Neither was it, when completed, the most viable film. It was 'death' at the box office. In fact, an 'artistic' film, faithful to the original story (which is how I set out to direct it before I was stopped), could not have taken less at the box office – and would most likely have made more.

In my time, I have given some of today's names in the world of entertainment their first big chance: Tony Britton, Janet Munro, Julie Andrews, Roger Moore were but a few of them. In the first musical I directed, *Everybody Cheer*, there were two 'unknowns'; Jean Carr, later the film star Jean Kent, and Buddy Dunn who went on to become old 'grandfather' Clive Dunn.

Yvonne Mitchell, of course, had been an actress for some years. It was only when she won the *Daily Mail* Award for the Year's Best Television Actress in three plays that I directed in rapid succession for BBC TV, that she became thought of as a 'star'. These plays brought her into the wider public view and gained her acclaim.

Roger Moore, aided and abetted by his then wife, Dorothy Squires, managed to land an audition for a part in *A Pin to See the Peepshow*, when that play was produced in New York. I was able, having tested him earlier at half a dozen auditions, to engage him; once he had been shown the rudiments of acting, he was soon snapped up by the films. I do not think he has ever been quite so good as he was in that particular play. As a stage presence then, he was young, manly, absolutely fresh, and he played the handsome young lover of Julia Almond (Edith Thompson) with a rare, brazen manner, and necessary gaucheness.

Prior to our meeting, Julie Andrews had been part of a three-cornered musical act, in variety (with her father and mother, Ted and Barbara Andrews), and a principal girl in pantomime for Emile Littler. When I was casting for *Mountain Fire*, it was Julie Andrews who landed the part of the leading girl, the only member of the cast who danced, played and sang. As this was a play with music and not only a musical, Julie was urgently required to *act*. It is interesting to note that she was taught how to act by Joan Miller.

The show never made it to the West End although it could have come in at the end of its pre-London tour and transferred to the Strand Theatre. However, Julie had been seen in Leeds, during the play's try-out tour, by two American impresarios. They were over here talent-spotting, and when *Mountain Fire* failed to make it to the West End, they cast her as a very 'English' actress in *The Boy Friend*, on Broadway. Later, being 'on the spot' in New York, she was instantly thought of as the perfect Eliza in Moss Hart's original Broadway production of *My Fair Lady*. The rest we know. Rex Harrison was Higgins, Stanley Holloway, Doolittle. It was a rave, and when it came to this country two years after its New York run had finished, it ran another two years at Drury Lane.

I was sitting in the stalls on that first night in 1955, and afterwards in an euphoric atmosphere went backstage with Joan and Arnold Goodman (now Lord Goodman, CH) then a partner in an established firm of Gray's Inn solicitors, and already a friend. Goodman by name, good man by nature, 'Goodie' to me he will always be. Julie stopped the animated congratulatory conversation in her dressing room when she saw us, by holding up her hand and announcing, 'I owe all *this* to Peter Cotes.' I would far rather that she had said, 'I owe all this to Joan Miller.' However, it was said in the general excitement of the moment, and it was thoughtful for the new world star to give credit at all. Later Julie was to become the wife of the American producer,

Blake Edwards, and gain further international stardom in *Mary Poppins* and *The Sound of Music*. It is doubtful whether any further thoughts occurred about earlier 'stepping stones'. Certainly, when Julie came to write an account of her life years later, she failed to spend even a paragraph on discussing the musical play that really started off her international career as a world star.

Mountain Fire was a lucky production for two other people: Gillian Lynne (choreographer of *Cats*, amongst others) had a part in it besides doing the choreography, and the front-of-house photographs were taken by a young unknown, Antony Armstrong-Jones, in his first professional assignment. I was happy to offer it to him, having visited his Pimlico studio and seen his early work when his father, Ronald Armstrong-Jones who was a friend of ours, had taken me there. The future Lord Snowdon, just down from university, was at the time setting up as a theatrical photographer (he had made a start on the royals already), and now this was to be his first production in the theatre.

Even so, myths grow and later, when an established star, Julie was alleged to have been a dancer and singer but no *actress*. As late as March 1992, the *Daily Telegraph* magazine wrote:

> So untutored was she in the art of acting that Moss Hart, the director, had to drill her in an 'intense weekend' of private tuition, bullying her just like a Professor Higgins. The lyricist, Alan Jay Lerner, made the artist/model connection: 'You must imagine Julie as a magnificent piano, with a marvellous tone, capable of producing great beauty but the keys wouldn't strike themselves. Moss knew how to draw out the fine music'.

Nevertheless, *Mountain Fire* and Joan Miller between them gave Julie the much needed groundwork that enabled her to tackle Eliza in *My Fair Lady* when it erupted onto the Broadway stage less than two years after *Mountain Fire* closed.

Pictures in the Fire

*The trouble with my looking glass
is that it shows me, me.
There's trouble in all sorts of things
where it should never be*

Mervyn Peake

No Star Nonsense became required reading at a number of American and Australian universities who provided theatre studies courses. The publishers were delighted when it won a 'Theatre World' award and was praised in print by such literary luminaries of the day as C.P. Snow, Pamela Hansford Johnson, F. Tennyson Jesse and John Brophy, among others.

The book was said to have shaken the theatrical establishment by propagating unfashionable ideas. Critics of the calibre of Ivor Brown (*The Observer*) and Harold Hobson (*The Sunday Times*) devoted their entire columns to discussing the merits of this book of ideas, ideas which had been generated for some years past in my own little theatres.

The theatres I ran in London and Manchester were unique in one respect: they generally were liked by those who admired small theatres, but most surprising perhaps was the fact that even theatre managers were interested. Managers are less prone than average theatre-goers to favour enterprises run on the proverbial shoestring. In small theatres a profit is hard to make except through the odd transfer to bigger theatres in the West End. An audience has to feel bowled over by the entertainment on hand in order to overlook the cramped and pokey conditions of most of today's fringe theatres.

I have always found small stages a challenge to ingenuity, limiting as they do the possibilities of more expensive décor. The movements and groupings of the actors become crucial to the ultimate realization of perfect stagecraft. Against these objections, artistic as well as financial, stands an important fact of theatre history, impossible to deny. Some of the most impressive productions and performances have been given in small theatres, sometimes on postage-stamp-sized stages, the 'event' of *Rosmersholm* a classic case in point. This production had a superb cast, David Markham, Esme Percy and Kynaston Reeves, and a central performance by Joan Miller as Rebecca West. This miniature production, with hardly any scenery to help it, took its place as the type of majestic piece that happens 'once in a blue moon'. I was told by Desmond MacCarthy in the pages of *The New Statesman*: 'You must go and see her (Joan) on the stage and experience the living presence of her.' Joan had already brought her unique gift to the art of sound broadcasting, and seasons in rep at Birmingham helped. She appeared later in such radio productions as *The Dark River*, *Ram in the Thicket*, *The Same Sky*, *Anna Christie* and *All My Sons*; to mention but a few is to clutch at a mere handful of those many plays which she dignified with her vocal presence. Her *Marie Curie*, a sound radio triumph, was written and produced by Nesta Pain, a friend of many years and arguably the BBC's best talent.

It was in the theatre, however, that Joan brought every facet of her massive talent to bear, making great scripts greater and poor scripts better. To write about one's wife as a husband, and one's leading actress as a director, is well-nigh impossible. Certainly nothing I say here, or even later, will do her real justice as an actress, nor express the deep love and admiration I felt for her as a woman.

In my earlier book I compiled a list of plays, performances and productions that had much moved me as a spectator: 'pictures in the fire'. Many of my most exciting play-going experiences have been in small theatres. As that dedicated critic, Eric Shorter, has written:

> a spectator is as subject to atmosphere in a theatre as the director, the players or the playwright. Indeed the spectator helps to make that atmosphere much more than many spectators realise.

Yes, indeed, but only after the atmosphere being created for any audience can be transmitted in turn to the production itself. One notes this from empty theatres when final dress rehearsals are under way. Two of my past productions, Wilfrid Lawson in *The Father* at the little Arts, and Joan Miller in *A Pin to See the*

Peepshow at the even smaller New Boltons, can be counted acting triumphs for the artists concerned. Yet, although Joan's and Willy's performances were both startling pieces of bravura acting at its most blazing, even in empty auditoriums,* it was when their intensity was rewarded with the 'sound of silence' emanating from an enthralled live audience, that the full impact of that 'kick-of-a-horse' sensation was made. One was a one-set, eight-character piece, the other had a cast of twenty-two and twelve changes of scenery. Yet the effects they had on audiences were identical.

The small theatres of London, the Ambassadors, the Duke of York's, the Duchess and one or two others outside, at Hammersmith, Hampstead and Islington, should all be encouraged as venues for certain types of drama and tragedy. They are big enough to count as centres of sometimes rare enterprise. Likewise, they often cultivate and encourage new playwrights. Small theatres are often off the beaten track, or, because of a reputation for taking risks, attract the sort of audience that will itself take a risk. These audiences, albeit small, will not wait for a play's box-office success and acceptance by the critics, before seeing it. In fact an audience comprised of such playgoers as these small theatre regulars might well wish to be there first, before the others, critics and larger public alike, have got wind of it.

If you look at the histories and origins of new movements in the theatre in the present century, you will detect the role of small playhouses. Sometimes they were so small that not more than several hundred at a time might have gathered, sometimes fewer than that, to fill the auditorium with expectation. There is today no lack of fringe theatre (to judge by certain presentations there may actually be far too many). There is, however, a lack of the small theatres in the West End for housing the more intimate type of entertainment. What room can be found today to shelter yesterday's fringe, the small theatre movement of even a score of years ago?

---

*In an empty theatre was how critic J.C. Trewin judged the worth of *A Pin to See the Peepshow*, and Queen Mary, too, when she commanded a special performance of *Pick-Up Girl*.

My first book, *No Star Nonsense* contained a number of pen-portraits of people I had known and admired. There were some reasonable things in it, despite, or perhaps because of, the white-hot heat of passion in which it was written. The portrait of Harley Granville-Barker was described by the then *Manchester Guardian* as more lifelike than anything in the authorized biography. And there can be no doubt that the chapters The Actor, The Producer, The Critic and The Theatrical Agent, were occasionally as light-hearted as they were impertinent. But a young man of the theatre, with any individuality in him, ought to be impertinent at times, and humble when in the presence of true talent. Humility, however, is not much in evidence in today's theatre.

In reading that first book now, perhaps it is not the impertinence to which I take exception, but the reverence. In a few of the pages that now follow I shall deal with some of the folk who came to have an influence upon my varied, chequered, and often eventful career.

I cannot wholly recognize the man of yesterday who wrote that book. He appears to be, here and there, a different type of 'animal' to any I know today. The truth is that nearly every year shifts the angle of one's outlook. Yet none of the basic conclusions need too much retraction now.

Perhaps it is wrong to dislike the attitude of people who praise the past at the expense of the present, even when looking back is sometimes therapy to those who feel genuinely lost without the comfort of their past emotions. Today such a feeling is called nostalgia. I am disinclined to eulogize too freely even those most splendid players whose interpretations gave me untold pleasure at a time when I was most susceptible to such 'sea breezes'. I think Maggie Smith and such present-day actors as Alison Steadman, Alec McCowen, Juliet Stevenson, Nigel Hawthorne and Eileen Atkins, can be as talented as the choice actors of my youth. They who were filled with joy, strength, power of conviction, and had fine elocution; this latter, a virtue in its day, but nowadays almost an unknown quality, when we are frequently fed through mechanical amplifiers. Audiences constantly suffer difficulty in hearing what all the mumblers and mincers are whispering and screaming about.

The standard of acting when, say, a Jacky MacGowran is around, can be as high today as in the past; even so, the stage that's past, with its spectacular bravura performances, is rarely exceeded in quality.

Bernard Shaw wrote of Forbes-Robertson's Hamlet that 'Nothing quite so charming has been seen by this generation. It will bear seeing again and again'. The reverse could equally be said about Wilfrid Lawson's Captain in Strindberg's *The Father*. He made the role the most credible, if charmless, monster I have ever seen in the part. The madness, the dangerous menace, the stature of the man – all had to be seen to be believed. But why do we make the comparison in the first place? Perhaps because in Forbes-Robertson we have the perfect formal actor, whereas in Lawson we search in vain for any formality whatsoever.

In the 1880s Sir Henry Irving gave a lecture at Harvard University on the 'Art of Acting'. We can detect in this piece, more than a century later, an allusion to that special something possessed by both Henry Irving and Wilfrid Lawson.

The immortal part of the stage is its nobler part. Ignoble accidents and interludes come and go but this lasts for ever. It lives like the human soul in the body of humanity, associated with much that is inferior and hampered by many hindrances, but never sinks into nothingness. It never fails to find new and noble work in creations of permanent and memorable excellence.

And I would say as a last word to the young men in this assembly who may at any time resolve to enter the dramatic profession, that they ought always to fix their minds upon the highest example. That in studying acting they should beware prejudiced comparisons between this method and that, but learn as much as possible from all. They should remember that art is as varied as nature, and as little suited to the shackles of a school. Above all they should never forget that excellence in any art is attained only by arduous labour, unswerving purpose and unfailing discipline.

To much of Irving's lecture, Willy would have pulled faces and made rude noises, but like it or not he was one of the 'greats' who, from time to time, came lurching along the highway, through the stage door, or onto any platform that passes for a stage, making 'make-believe' more exciting and, while it lasts, the theatre a better place in which to perform.

Going to the 'Fumes'

A proper Mrs Malaprop our Grannie was

I was born at Maidenhead, which between the wars was a charming Berkshire marketing town on the river with a tiny population. My brothers, John and Roy, were born there too, at Bray, a mere two miles away, at the home of an aunt. They stuck to our family name, Boulting. All of us were close together in age, but they were *exactly together*, having been born identical twins. Our youngest brother, Guy, died when young of meningitis. We had one thing in common: we were all 'filmstruck' as kids. Living first in one house by the river at Maidenhead, and subsequently at Taplow, we made frequent visits to the two principal picture-palaces in the town. The Queen Street Cinema was situated at one end of Maidenhead High Street, and the Picture House was located at the other end, over Maidenhead Bridge.

As I remember, it was the owner of the former, Mr Wright, who was the better known character of the two cinema proprietors. In those days, without there being any syndicates to worry about, individuality was in the saddle. Mr Wright was generally called 'Old Father Wright' behind his back, although I doubt whether the rather formal Mr Wright, in his sober grey suit, was ever young! He sat in his box office dealing out those metal discs that passed for paper tickets for the 6ds, 10ds and 1/3ds. And I vividly remember Mr Goodey at the Picture House, before spotted bow-ties became all the rage. He always wore one, and this was a good thirty years or so before the Robin Day television era. Mr Goodey was to be seen waiting in the entrance to his cinema, a figure of sartorial respectability, who, unlike his rival, Mr Wright, was always faultlessly attired in a dark blue suit. In fact, I don't think I ever saw Goodey in anything but blue, nor Wright in anything but grey.

However, I do remember distinctly that the best films were always screened at the Bridge Street venue, though an occasional 'big' film was shown at the Queen Street house. The musical accompaniment was superior at the Picture House, too, and the projectionist there seemed a bit more professional. True, at Queen Street one could see all the popular cowboy stars; William S. Hart, Buck Jones, Hoot Gibson and Ruth Roland in serials and most of the Tom Mix and 'Tony' features. But there was no 'barring clause' for Mix and some of his best 'fumes' were always seen first at the Picture House. (My dear grandmother, a veritable 'Mrs Malaprop' in her day, had coined the term 'fumes', when she was describing the films she had seen. She disliked the violence of cowboy 'fumes' and preferred romances.)

There, and again at Brighton, later, I saw most of the early Chaplin films and eventually the first of the 'greats' by that same genius, such as *Shoulder Arms*, *The Pilgrim* and *The Kid*. By the time the Chaplin masterpieces of the twenties and the thirties were made, *The Gold Rush*, *The Circus*, *City Lights* and *Modern Times*, we had moved elsewhere. I was to see these films many times.

Later in life I was to write a book on Chaplin in collaboration with a friend, Thelma Niklaus, for which my admiration of Charlie stood by way of dedication:

> In memory of Sydney Bennett who through introducing the First Artist of the Screen to his precocious, emotional and affectionate grandchild, was directly responsible for what follows.

Fortunately, by the time we'd finished this study my associate had also become a fully fledged admirer of our subject. The book, *The Little Fellow*, was a big success when it was published; firstly by Elek, and later by the Bodley Head in 1951.

This was the year, too, when I met Charlie for the first time after many years of star-gazing. He was over in England (from which he never returned to the States) on a visit with his wife and family. It was the first of a number of meetings, which culminated in my being invited to stay with the Chaplins at the beautiful Swiss mansion, purchased when it was decided that he would never again return to that country where he had made his fame and fortune in the previous forty years of his life. And from where, through his wonderful films, he had made the whole world laugh.

I was later to record for the BBC, as a birthday tribute, details of my first meeting with Chaplin – on that occasion being treated to a performance of mimicry and mime that was indescribable and unforgettable for long after it lasted. I was on my own having tea in the suite on the River Room at the Savoy Hotel, and this solo performance by the Little Fellow could not have been bought for 'all the tea in China'. And it was put on just for me. That 'interview' should, today, be in the BBC archives.

Sadly, much later I was to talk about Charlie Chaplin in a recorded BBC obituary. My memories of the man and the artist were used in the first programme ever to be transmitted from Broadcasting House of the subsequently long-running feature, 'Kaleidoscope' (then produced by Rosemary Hart).

He was eighty-eight when he finally died, for years the best known Londoner in the world – at one time the best known comedian in the world. Chaplin, the screen's greatest actor. Charlie, the greatest of all clowns. Few success stories can compare with that of the street urchin from Kennington who at the age of eleven was still unable to read and write but who became before he was thirty the most celebrated film artist of them all.

His greatest creative achievement was to produce a self-portrait, a direct and astonishing expression of himself, and that factor gave fluidity to all his films. If we are to appreciate the consistency of his truly marvellous performances during a life that was theatrical from the start and spanned well over seventy years, it is necessary to bear his background constantly in mind. As a child he suffered the loneliness of a waif. When his mad mother (his father was an alcoholic) was removed from their poor home he suffered penury, sleeping under street arches with his brother Syd, sustaining himself with garbage from the plates of others. He was admitted to Hanwell workhouse and was later dominated by the twin themes, bread, and loneliness and a hatred of organized society.

Such obsessions haunt all his major works, from *The Tramp* (1915) to *Monsieur Verdoux* (1947). The funniest man in the world, he was at the same time the saddest. He was much more than the great clown, with his superlative miming, brilliant acting, talented musicianship and wild acrobatics; the eternal Peter Pan, he 'showed off' in little dances rivalling the movement of Nureyev. In the films of his time, none of the 'giants' – Tati, Garbo, Keaton, Valentino, Dressler – could ever hold a candle to him, nor hold the attention with a fraction of the intensity belonging to the Little Fellow. The first satirical film I ever remember seeing was a brilliantly innovatory Chaplin two-reeler, *The Immigrant*, from the 1920s, in which huddled immigrants, Charlie among them, look out from a tramp steamer at the Statue of Liberty and their overcrowded cargo boat enters the land of the free. Lubitsch's *The Marriage Circle*, considered by many to be, with Chaplin's *A Woman of Paris*, the first satirical picture, came only years later.

Chaplin could at any time have moved along more detached paths but luckily for us the spirit proved irresistible and a series of masterpieces was the result. And what a list! One remembers with pleasure and fascination films such as *One A.M.*, *The Pawn Shop*, *The Cure* and *The Count* (how many times have we all enjoyed these?), after which there followed *Sunnyside*, then the first of the masterpieces, *Shoulder Arms*, and *The Kid*.

When we come to the films that followed – my favourite film critic, Dilys Powell, has always remembered to include references to his films in her list of the 'greats' – we seem to be entering into an experience that was 'other-worldly'. In *City Lights* and *Modern Times* we are taken to the highest peaks of motion-picture art. Chaplin did for films what Chekhov did for drama; like the Russian, our cockney hero had a lovable simplicity that went straight to the heart. No one, not even the professionals, can explain the joy in a Chaplin film. There are some who are cursed by a compulsion to 'explain' comedy, to try to elucidate the little matter of jokes, why films are funny, how comedy is serious. Nothing is more exhausting than this tendency, when by its very nature comedy is inexplicable. Mel Brooks – not a very funny man as a comic, better as a comedy writer-director – defines comedy as 'the opposite of tragedy. Tragedy is if I twist *my* ankle, comedy is if you fall down a sewer and die.' Exactly. But it still leaves *why*? It is a thing of wonder that we don't need to analyze any more than we do the Taj Mahal or Beethoven's Ninth. Sam Goldwyn called him 'the greatest artist of the lot, the best we never had', and Bernard Shaw was of the opinion that 'Chaplin was the only genius developed in motion pictures'.

Chaplin's films when talkies came did not falter. His *Great Dictator, Monsieur Verdoux* and *Limelight* were all works of cinematic art, and although the last two pictures he made over here were disappointing – an old man's self-indulgence – they did have hilarious sequences.

In the millions of words written about Charlie Chaplin – constructive, denigrating, loving and sometimes hating (for what artist has not had his detractors?) – perhaps the epitaph that must stand as the best is Colin Hurry's, displaying as it does the poet's comic muse at its best:

He'll catch St. Peter unawares before the trumpet's blown,
He'll tumble up the golden stairs and trip before the throne,
He'll greet the cherubims with chaff, and when the skies are riven
With echoes of their comic laugh, his sins will be forgiven.

I remember Maidenhead for reasons other than the cinemas and 'fumes'. Boulters Lock on an Ascot Sunday; Skindles Hotel at weekends in the spring and summer; and 'in season', the then Prince of Wales ('Prince Charming', they called him) dancing at Murray's River Club, one of the country's first, and best known out-of-town night clubs. There is, however, no memory from my childhood I hold so dear as that of going to the 'flicks' (the Americanized word 'movies' came later). I usually went with my old grandfather, less frequently with my brothers. Roy and John used to play around a great deal with toy cinemas that they made out of paper, glue and cardboard. In our time the Queen Street Cinema was popularly known (not always unkindly) as 'Old Wrights's Gaff'. This name was derived without doubt from that derisive term applied to some of the very early music halls and fleapits: 'the penny gaffs'. 'Father' Wrights's prices were higher than that, except when he was competing with Mister Goodey for the children's matinée custom on Saturday mornings, when the prices would sharply descend to the blessed halfpenny, which was at the time the same price I was able to pay at second-hand bookstalls and traders' barrows to start a library after having had a good browse through first.

I was an inveterate reader from childhood onwards. From *The Boys' Own Paper* I passed on to the standard story tales: 'Sapper', Wodehouse,* Conan Doyle, Dickens, Scott, and all the theatrical biographies, of course. In those days it was clearly all their own work. The modern fashion for having celebrity life stories 'ghosted' had not arrived, and one detected the truth of the lives of Mrs Aria, Mrs Pat, Lily Langtry, Tree, Irving, Ellen Terry, and, most of all perhaps, my own favourite, George Arliss's *On-Stage*. Later came the novels of Trollope, the Brontës and H.G. Wells, with such 'lowbrows' as Frank Richards, Rider Haggard and Hall Caine thrown in as escapism. I am afraid if I said how many books I read between the ages of twelve and twenty, many would think I was romancing. But I can definitely date the fact that long before I was twenty I was conversant with both Zola and Anatole France; Guy de Maupassant, Bernard Shaw, Ibsen and Thomas Hardy, too, were loves that never palled. Nor for that matter had I earlier missed out on the schoolboy yarns of Frank Richards, a pseudonym for one who wrote not only about Greyfriars but about St Jim's and Rookwood.

I think this voracious desire to read was aided by a number of things. The first was that I had nothing by way of obstruction. School-crammed, the mental soil was healthy where no weeds might choke the better growth. Secondly I was a very rapid reader, so much so that I often had to demonstrate to others that I had actually read the matter before me. (I still possess that capacity, very little weakened, and I can by a glance through a new book, tell if the work is worth bothering with or not. I have a very tenacious memory where books, plays, speeches and music are concerned, and I am generally able to tell where a passage is to be found, even going so far as to photograph in my mind whether it was on a left or a right hand page, and whether at the top or the bottom.) Finally I did not *have* to read, there was no compulsion, no having to work through a subject. It was a

---

*In the mid 1960s, I produced with the BBC the first TV series of stories by P.G. Wodehouse ever allowed to be shown anywhere in the world. Bertie Wooster was played by Ian Carmichael and Jeeves by Dennis Price. Titled 'The World of Wooster', it was an instantaneous success that led to further series on both television and radio, and has since been seen on TV in further series still, with Hugh Laurie and Stephen Fry as the inimitable pair.

question of reading what I wanted to, when I wanted to, and for so long as I was interested enough to keep on reading. Such things make the devil of a difference. I hope this will not be considered boasting if I offer it as an explanation of how I managed to get through so much in so short a time.

I have known personally a great many writers of note in my time and remember with admiration and often affection such authors as C.P. Snow, Pamela Hansford Johnson, John Brophy and his talented daughter, Brigid, Charles Rodda (who wrote superior thrillers under the pseudonym 'Gavin Holt' and to whom Eric Ambler has long expressed his indebtedness); the talented novelist and editor of so many notable British trials, F. Tennyson Jesse and her playwright husband, H.M. Harwood; the American, Lillian Hellman – secretly much criticized during her lifetime and openly maligned since her death; J.B. ('Jolly Jack') Priestley, as well as scores of others. Nesta Pain and Julian Symons are valued friends – highly talented and versatile, both of them. I rubbed up against others as a boy when my parents took me to see them as their close friends: Henry St John Cooper (brother of actress Gladys Cooper) and his wife, Cis. Cis was an eccentric 'good sort', large and gin-soaked, who often boasted that she'd sank many a ship – and would go on doing so if the sea remained alcoholic! Her husband found her good copy for his books and romantic serials that were for many years avidly consumed by readers of the old *Daily Mirror*, long before that other romantic novelist, Barbara Cartland, was ever heard of.

No list of mine should exclude the larger-than-life Swiss novelist, John Knittel, who made a huge reputation and fortune between the wars with such best-selling novels on the continent of Europe as *Thérèse Raquin* and *Via Mala*; the latter the story of a big Swiss mountain, and a family of peasants within its shadow, from which I adapted a stage play which was eventually seen on the English stage under the title *So Wise, So Young* (borrowed from the Bard, of course). This was the 1960s and the cast included Joan Miller, Emrys Jones, Mary Yeomans, Andrew Ray and Fiona Duncan. It did well in a number of important cities, but not well enough to take into the West End. We grew to know Knittel and his large and interesting family well – his wife, Frances, an Englishwoman, had his three children (two daughters, and a son who became a partner in two English firms of publishers, Cape, and later Collins). One daughter, Margaret – beautiful and hugely talented as both painter and musician – played the piano on several occasions as soloist for the Hallé Orchestra under Sir John Barbirolli and married a relative of the German conductor, Wilhelm Furtwängler.

'Big John' was by far the most outsize character I knew in my gallery of literary friends, although neither Osbert nor Edith Sitwell should be neglected mention. I came to know Osbert through Joan, who first met him in the war years whilst appearing at Birmingham's Alexandra Theatre in repertory.

Early in her career, Joan's appearance in the title role of *The Tzarina* (a play adapted by R. J. Minney from Sitwell's novel, *Gentle Caesar*) led to a visit from Osbert and an enduring correspondence between actress and novelist. The latter subsequently became an ardent admirer and regular member of any first-night audience when his 'favourite actress' – as he called Joan – was appearing.

Upon one occasion, two Sitwells appeared instead of the usual one, in Joan's dressing room after the performance of *Staring at the Sun*, at the Vaudeville Theatre in the West End. Osbert had brought Edith backstage with him, and after her brother's congratulatory greeting his sister, The Dame, held the floor. The talk, for no good reason that Joan could see, was steered by Edith in the direction of the respective merits of Shaw and Wells (G.B.S., perhaps, because Osbert had seen Joan early in her career as Mrs Dubedat and later as Candida – but why Wells remained a mystery!). I recall Joan telling me after this visit how she had 'taken against' Sister Edith when the latter airily dismissed Wells with a 'Thank God HGW never wrote plays', to which Joan had innocently replied, 'Well, we're in *his* debt for writing novels so outstandingly down the years'. Quick as a flash, Edith retorted 'Well, Shaw at least was a gentleman and Wells wasn't'.

Joan always possessed opinions of her own and told me afterwards of this snobbish as well as glaring *non sequitur* with disapproval, and how she had refused to be anything but polite to this far from easy guest. However, it was clear that Osbert shifted uncomfortably in his chair and smiled as he caught

Joan's look of incredulity. He had been witness to many similar remarks made by his sister and grown to accept, without endorsing, her snobby points of view.

I have seen so many plays, films and listened to good music as well as cheap, but perhaps my greatest need of all was for books. I wanted them to be my own. I could never get the full benefit from a book I had to borrow. I could write a whole chapter on the many devices by which I built up a library: haunting stalls and second-hand furniture shops (the book hunter should never miss these), where I picked up many prizes. They had to be inexpensive, but I was evidently born with a nose for books, for it was in this way I came to make the acquaintance of some of the world's best writers. Odd volumes were to me almost as welcome as complete sets, and then not so very cheap at 2d or 3d. I made the acquaintance of many great historians by way of an odd volume, and later found philosophy, Russell and Ayer especially, to be my ticket. Visiting second-hand book sellers and browsing is a favourite occupation, and should be recommended rather than going without in order to buy an expensive book. In my opinion many publishers today seem to have turned highwaymen, and publish books at anything from £10 to £30. They must be putting their product out of the reach of so many who would like to read more. I have rarely envied others their possessions, whatever they were, unless they had a well-stocked library. Then, I must confess, I could not suppress a strong feeling that many of their books would look better on my shelves than they did on their own.

I am not, alas, very methodical in my readings, and I collect all too many references, and make all too many notes. I have a very strong conviction that ten minutes of interested reading is far more profitable than a couple of hours reading where interest is lacking or weak. I found, however, the advantage gained by making notes; and attempting to file those notes under the proper headings; yet that advantage was discounted by not being able to find the notes when I wanted them! To make the picture complete I must also say that I have usually read with no specific purpose in view. Of course when I came across anything that interested me, or I was deliberately seeking an explanation of something, I might follow the trail from one book to another, until I had got some sort of an answer. I browse as I read, picking out things that may one day come in useful.

'Browsing' is fascinating, and one forgets the present in a past of received pictures. It was J.M. Barrie's Peter Pan who cried 'first impressions are very important'. First sounds are unforgettable too, especially when they remind you of some of the first sights you ever had. John Crook's evocative music for *Peter Pan* is also unforgettable. I was to play in *Peter Pan* as a boy actor: three different parts, John, Slightly and Starkey, in three different professional productions, after a training at the then famous Italia Conti Stage School. Once upon a time, the play *Peter Pan* had music as important to its production as the Tenniel drawings were to the book of *Alice in Wonderland*.

'How potent cheap music is', was Noël Coward's rather snobby reply to melody for the masses. One heard it in the thirties, when put over so memorably by Gertrude Lawrence in Coward's own play *Private Lives*. Some of this so called *cheapest*, can be the most potent when it is as good as 'Some Day I'll Find You'.

I was brought up on the music of the music halls. 'Potent', most of it; Souza marches from the pit orchestra at the start, and usually waltzes by Strauss, Tchaikovsky, and Hermann Finck in the intervals. Sidney Baynes was another universal musical provider for conjurers, trapeze artists, jugglers, acrobats, illusionists, and the rest of those graceful performers who did tricks with mime, and needed just that type of 'background' music produced by his evocative waltz, 'Destiny'. I've never forgotten the sound and the smell of the 'cheap', 'potent' music of my youth; with its memory invoking not only Houdini, Maskelyne and Devant, Conrad and his Pigeons but also Albert Whelan, the Australian entertainer as well. Whelan in top hat, white tie and tails, would make a grand first entrance, whistling the whole time. Silver-knobbed black stick under arm, he'd saunter down a darkened centre-stage, a white spotlight following him before he languidly removed his white gloves. Rolled together, he would nonchalantly drop them into his opera hat, as he bowed with his topper held on heart. Finally, completing his walk to the foot lights, he would stop centre down stage, and say to his audience, 'Good evening'. The stage was ablaze with light, and audience applause lit up the auditorium. 'The Jolly Woodman' was the theme tune for this piece of well-remembered mime.

This was all 'conjurers' music if you like, and together with the rousing ditties heard in music hall, revue, and musical comedy stages between the wars, they've gone on to stay with us long after the Second World War. One such romantic ballad from the Bing Boys in the First World War has been recorded umpteen times. And many singers, poles apart, including Streisand, Sinatra, and Garland have featured it down the years. But when I wrote a BBC 'Omnibus' tribute for Norman Swallow to mark the centenary of George Robey a few years ago, it was to none of the present day stars I went for the best version of Nat D. Ayer's lovely old duet. No, it was to the two original artists, and a recording in the BBC archives of Violet Loraine and George Robey singing 'If You Were the Only Girl in the World'.

'Cheap' music, perhaps, 'potent' music, most certainly. And once, when working with the late Sir John Barbirolli, he told me of the pleasure he derived when conducting many melodies that are sometimes looked down upon by the musical snobs.* 'Glorious John' showed his disdain for those he termed "highbrows without hearts', by frequently playing waltzes and marches by Souza, Offenbach, Strauss and Lehar amongst others. And whilst swaying to Barbirolli playing Lehar, I was automatically set thinking of Charlie Chaplin. The conductor was a great admirer of the comedian, and some of that artist's distinctive compositions for a number of memorable films recall to me some time or happening in the past, that doesn't always appear to have a natural link with the melody.

A very different type of artist is almost forgotten today. Her best known song is associated more with others than with the actress herself. I first saw Elsie Janis, an American star of the

*I produced two television programmes starring the great conductor: 'The Rehearsal – Before and After', and 'Master of Music' (a life), both transmitted by Granada from Manchester's Free Trade Hall in 1958. In the latter, Evelyn Rothwell (Lady Barbirolli), the oboeist, made a charming appearance.

twenties, at the old Adelphi Theatre in the revue, *Clowns in Clover*, with Jack Hulbert and his wife, Cicely Courtneidge. The year was 1928. Ten years earlier she'd made a hit when introducing to London audiences the haunting number she created, 'Give Me the Moonlight', one that manages to linger on. Elsie Janis was also a wonderful impressionist, better than any I've seen since. Or is this only a 'first impression' I wonder? Elsie Janis was not merely like those she impersonated, she became them. Only one other mimic could hold a candle to her and that was my father. He would sit at the piano and, accompanying himself, make his family think that he was Eugene Stratton, Dan Leno, Herbert Campbell, Gus Elen, Arthur Roberts, R.G. Knowles, or 'Jolly' John Nash. There is of course nothing in any archive of my dear old dad, but his friend, Albert Chevalier (the one he admired more than any other artist and who used to visit us when we lived in Whitwell Road, Southsea), can still be heard in my memory now singing several of those numbers, such as 'Wot'cher', 'Our Little Nipper' and 'My Old Dutch', to which my father would often treat his youthful audience. They were two of the potent songs my parents taught me to appreciate when still a 'little nipper' myself. A long time ago now, but then, 'first impressions' are very important, don't you agree?

Brothers and Others

Oh what a lovely war!

As children, Roy and John were keenly aware of others, quiet and only occasionally tempestuous. Grown up, they were to become argumentative, provocative, and often irritating. Whichever adjective you pin to them, the Boulting Brothers as they were to become known, were only rarely humble, occasionally arrogant, never complacent and always unequivocal. They remained for nearly two score years (despite the never-ending publicity that accompanied them, both on film sets and in private), mystery men. They had hectic and controversial life-styles, moving in what were often conformist atmospheres. These atmospheres failed either to tame or stale them. They were born mimics, an inherited gift.

In the post-war years they became acknowledged masters of British screen comedy. They had started out, one as the proverbial tea-carrying assistant, the other as third assistant director, in a small B-picture film production company, which was headed by a gloriously eccentric and erratic character by the name of Widgey Newman. From such small beginnings did they rise, John entering Wardour Street from Reading School and Roy from education in the Navy on HMS *Worcester*.

As their own masters – a state of grace for which they fought desperately hard – they began by making serious films. Two of them, *Consider Your Verdict* and *Inquest* were produced on the proverbial 'shoe-string' without letting it show. Others, such as *Pastor Hall* and *Thunder Rock*, earned them exceptional press notices, as well as worldwide film distribution.

My brothers also earned the deep suspicion of the British film industry, which was controlled for most of their professional lives by two greedy and acquisitive giants, the Rank Organization and Associated British (formerly British International Pictures). These two fanned the flames of doubt concerning them, by continuously keeping that suspicion alive. In fact neither their long list of box office hits, nor their status as producers and members of the board of British Lion ever quite exorcized the raised-eyebrow view of them that prevailed in the cigar-perfumed boardrooms of Wardour Street.

With their trilogy of assaults on some of the country's best known sacred cows – *Private's Progress* (the Army), *I'm All Right Jack* (trade unions) and *Heavens Above!* (the Church of England) – they brought a fresh, impudent and irreverent approach to the world around them; the satire was barbed and its main targets suitably red-faced. *Brothers in Law* (the Law) and *Carlton-Browne* (the Foreign Office) were among others satirized to the point of no return.

Today satire is less fashionable, and not as popular as it was in the fifties and sixties. It persists nevertheless, with institutions and their guardians still being regularly lampooned, thanks perhaps to such talents as Alan Bennett and Dennis Potter. Long before such new waves of satire crashed on Britain's complacent shores, the screen (often regarded as the *derrière-garde* of the arts), in the shape of my brothers had got there first.

John and Roy, who had been prophetically nicknamed in their youth, 'Man of the World' and 'Gentleman', respectively (my own nickname had been 'Sporting Nib'!) had always been observant youngsters with retentive memories. They came in their professional lives to employ the unequalled weapon of laughter to mock and question the morality of the affluent society. In doing this they became affluent themselves, much married and world famous into the bargain.

When John died suddenly of cancer in 1985, the British Film Institute gave him a memorial tribute at the National Film Theatre which was attended by those who knew him as both man and producer. Dilys Powell and Graham Greene were among those speakers who recognized his achievements. Roy and I paid our own tributes to 'Man of the World', whose talents had given to the many who were present that night so much happiness in the past.

Today Roy, in his seventies, is writing the lives of the Boulting Twins, who made their own distinctive contribution to the screen after seeing their first 'fumes' long before talkies were born. Their war will doubtless be touched upon in Roy's lengthy narrative: enlistment, promotion, enhanced reputations, doing what they did best by making films for the war effort. Roy, in the Army film unit directed both *Desert Victory* and *Burma Victory*, whilst John, similarly commissioned in the RAF, directed and wrote *Journey Together*. Edward G. Robinson came over from Hollywood to appear in that film.

Unlike the Twins', my 'war', although not one through which heroes are made, was nevertheless quite eventful, due to my continually having to change course. This was partly due to temperament, partly by accident. Certainly I had an abiding nervous energy that drove me on, always attempting to do too many things at the same time. It was a force that acted as a catalyst, encouraging me to spread my net wide so that nothing was too big or too small for me to take on. Before the war, too, I acted, understudied, stage managed (essaying boys' roles as well as juvenile leads before such time as it was ripe for me to do so). *Her First Affaire* was *my* first affair of any consequence – in the star's dressing room of a very unstarry theatre in the North of England in the thirties. Unlike the theatre (the Royal at Blackburn, Lancs) the lady in question was a dazzler. No two ways about it. But 'no names, no kiss and tell' even at this late date. In the West End (the role had been played by the glamorous Zillah Bateman; other members of the cast had been such names as Henry Hewitt, Margery Binner, Jack Hobbs (no relation to the famous cricketer, but a well known handsome and hearty actor of the day) and Ellen Pollock, who is still alive and continuing as president of the Shaw Society.

Her First Affaire had had a reasonably successful run at the Duke of York's. Adapted by the prolific Frederick Jackson from the French into a type of English farce that was aimed to call much broad laughter from audiences, it had a single setting, a small cast and the cachet of a West End run behind it to encourage its management to take it on a tour of the smaller towns in the English provinces. For this purpose, a cast of provincial actors of reliable reputation were chosen to essay the roles of glamorous siren wife, absent-minded husband, eligible and handsome juvenile lead and a 'jolly hockey-stick' young woman for the occasional alternative love interest. There was a saucily depicted French maid in this typically decent, if stupid and unconventional, English household who was supposed to bring yet more latent sex into the open. In fact, the ingredients were the usual ones of farce between the wars (unless, that is, they were written by the old master, Ben Travers, who was well served by the Aldwych Theatre-team of remarkable farceurs: Lynn, Walls, Brough, Kove, Hare, Shotter and Batty, to name but a few of these crafty craftsmen and -women of unique quality).

Alas, the farce I was selected to play in on tour ('direct from its run at the Duke of York's theatre' proclaimed the posters) had neither the wit nor the situation comedy of Aldwych farce. They were stereotypes, all, with the exception of me playing the juve lead. A 'handsome hearty in his late twenties' was called for and I was still in my teens, and far from hale or hearty. Instead of gobbling up the female characters in the cast as the script intended, I was the proverbial lamb in sheep's clothing – an adolescent miscast who had wandered into the wrong production. If Young Woodley, the title role of John van Druten's celebrated piece, had fallen in love with his housemaster's wife, then it was equally true that I'd developed a pash (or thought I had, for such are the fevered imaginings of peculiar adolescents) for the leading lady – or for the sexy character she played in this farce – I was captivated by her, both on stage and off.

Why I was ever entrusted with the role remains a mystery to this day – one that I'm sure The Great Detective himself would have had difficulty in solving. Meant by the author to be a predator and more than a bit of a 'letch' – fascinated by women and fascinating to them, the plot called for much sex of that day to be hinted at by all, rather than accomplished. In this theatrical soufflé, I instead resembled a victim – and the glaring miscasting, through my general appearance, served to add another (and grossly wrong) dimension to a plot that became ersatz Ben Travers-farce, rather than a saucy slice of English domestic life from 'Gay Paree'. It might have been entertaining fare for the good citizenry of the North, but I doubt it – even so, there was an attempt to appeal to the section of the audience in those days that went in for nudge-nudge, wink-wink, and saw characters as stereotypes rather than human beings. Certainly, all characters, even when depicted as caricatures, must have a base of common sense: that's what makes the situation-comedy funny, and is the base upon which farces such as *Her First Affaire* are built. The fact that I was not type cast – the sole member of the cast who wasn't – threw the piece, and I became not the most popular of the company. . . .

However, on one occasion I found myself alone in the dressing-room of the attractive actress, my senior by ten years at least. After the show that night, the same lady, sipping gin-and-french (that was her customary order to her dresser for curtain-fall), looked at me over the rim of her glass, and realizing that I had grown infatuated with her character, kissed me full on the mouth! I suppose she meant to make a man of me, even if it was only for the sake of the stage performances we were to play together for the rest of the tour! Certainly, for my part (whatever *her* reasons) I took it seriously, and there was no going back to my former calf-like self, after that first 'initiation' in a now empty backstage theatre. The rest of the cast had departed. Every night after the show I went in for my gin-and-french, (which in later life became a drink I lost much interest in) and our theatre life became all beer-and-skittles while it lasted. Looking back now to the scenes I played both on-stage and in dressing-room, I find it difficult to fathom what was real, what was false – impersonating the man in front of a chortling audience twice nightly, or being an infatuated adolescent out of stage-costume, bereft of his love lines in the charged atmosphere of an actress's dressing room.

How different today, so many years later, when anything goes, offstage and on, when what once passed for romance is now, in reality, adolescent titillation, and there is no longer a meaning attached to the word 'flirtation'. . . .

Later, apart from acting, I wrote and adapted stage plays for television and contributed sketches to revues. I sang and danced and acted as assistant to such directors as Leslie Henson in musicals and Irene Hentschel in straight plays. This was my life before, during and for some years after the war. This drive to try *anything* led to my taking a crack at a piece of film 'direction' given me when perhaps the chump who directed the scene should have known better. It led to an 'accident' that broke my neck and as it took place only a short time prior to the outbreak of war it was to affect me for the duration.

I was filming in a piece titled *Alibi* at the Gainsborough Studios, Islington. It starred Margaret Lockwood and James Mason and my role, that of a murder victim, contained a *hurtling* sequence in more ways than one. The incident that caused me so much pain, and others so much embarrassment, was later recalled by the actor-dramatist, Rodney Ackland, who was one of the two murderers in the plot. We had been rehearsing a scene in which the murderer pushed me through a trap-door in the 'flies' (the space above the stage), and had got through it once without mishap. But our director, Brian Desmond Hurst, felt that the scene had not been realistic enough. In his autobiography, *The Celluloid Mistress* Ackland remembers how nearly his push came to putting paid to my account forever:

> We took up our positions. On the word I pushed Peter and this time, unfortunately, he fell head first on to the mattress and he lay horribly still. 'Oh my God! I've killed him', I thought. Fortunately Peter was not dead – but he had broken his neck. He spent six months in plaster and seemed to recover from his gruesome experience: I imagine, though, that he wanted to forget it. . . .

Many years later I was again to be associated (successfully!) with Rodney Ackland, when I presented and directed the first West End revival for over thirty years of his play *The Old Ladies*. It co-starred Joan Miller, Joyce Carey and Flora Robson (and it turned out to be Robson's last West End appearance).

That glorious comedian, Robb Wilton had a catch-phrase, 'The day that war broke out' – and that was how I felt when I finally emerged some weeks later from St Leonard's Hospital, Hackney. I had been rushed there as a recumbent form on a stretcher, with spinal concussion. On my release I set about immediately making plans to volunteer for service in the Territorial Army, such was my state of mind and that ever-present nervous energy already noted.

The Queen's Westminster Rifles was my first port of call. Their base at the time was down near Victoria Street, a large empty drill hall. Here a number of actors known to me, some with whom I had worked in the past – Frank Lawton, Guy

Middleton, Hugh Williams, Nigel Patrick, Bob Coote and Michael Trubshaw – were already hard at it, all looking like younger members of what later became known as 'Dad's Army'. They drilled on odd days and nights during the long, frustrating period that came later to be known as 'the phoney war'. I had in fact some weeks before the accident, attempted to volunteer when the signs were plain that war was impending. Now, accepting my application to join the regiment I was, nevertheless, warned 'not to give up any employment you might have outside National Service'. To make sure that this warning was taken seriously my Certificate of Registration (which I still have) made a point of stating the fact.

Still shaken from the past weeks and not mobile enough yet to drill with the others, I accepted a stage engagement. I was to display my versatility by playing a number of cameo roles in sketches (fortunately *no* dancing) in a new revue that was going into rehearsal at the Q Theatre, Kew Bridge. It had a star cast of that time, including Hermione Baddeley and Henry Kendall, and a lot of other clever people in support, including little Joan Greenwood (not known to many at the time as one of Jacob Epstein's foremost child models) in what must have been one of her first stage engagements. The name of the show was *Rise Above It* and it was played at Kew first. The war situation being what it was the show did not come into the blacked-out West End just then, although it did later (at The Comedy) when it was all clear, and proved a hit. Chaplin's anti-Hitler film *The Great Dictator*, had recently opened and as propaganda against the enemy it could hardly have been bettered. A sketch I wrote titled *The Great Dictator*, where I dressed up as Charlie, was soon placed in the revue's running order and proved a big success. As it was mime it caused me little manual effort and, although I was no Marcel Marceau, audiences seemed to like what they saw, so this little cameo was retained for the run. One wished that everything one did could have proved so easy.

The beguiling Baddeley ('Totie' as she was invariably nicknamed), with whom I was to work so often in the future, was a great artist in revue (so in vogue between the wars) and seemed forever young. I knew her for the last forty years of her life, during which time she never seemed to age. She invited me, after our first revue together, to go on tour with her in a season of variety at, of all places, Blackpool! The war was still only rumbling in the distance, and Blackpool's salty summer audiences, unlike those in the wartime West End were surprisingly enthusiastic for this sophisticated star. I was only assisting Totie and keeping the stage inhabited with a few impersonations – including one of Randolph Sutton – while she was changing. I was described in the programme as her assistant and as we hit it off, both onstage and off, I can look back upon a long association with warm memories.

After touring a few selected dates we returned to a blacked-out West End. However, there again we immediately played together in a hastily improvized midnight revue in a renovated cellar somewhere below Lisle Street, Leicester Square. The 'Club', almost opposite the stage-door of the London Hippodrome, became known as 'The Nightlight' and was run by a sporty lady called Vi Dean. She managed to collect quite a few stars of West End revue ('my out-of-works', she called them) and apart from Totie we again had Joan Greenwood and such fashionable West End artistes of the day as Wilfrid Hyde White, Georgie Cookson, Hedley Briggs, Virginia Winter and Walter Crisham, as fellow and sister 'nightlights'. The bombs fell, but with our songs, dances and sketches (I was now 'feeding' Willy as well as Totie), we sent our dawn-breaking revellers away each morning tired but happy.

There were still no signs from my National Service masters, so when Totie asked me yet again to join her in a big city tour of a new revue I readily agreed. It was to be presented by Jack Waller (of *No, No, Nanette* and *Hit the Deck* fame) and titled *Hearts Are Trumps* – a jolly title for a rumbustious show. I, of course, had to warn the management that I might have to be called away. But Jack Waller was a gambler, and took the risk, I suspect, largely due to Totie's promotion of her chum. There were a number of other well-known 'names' in the cast of the new show, including Alfred Drayton, Wylie Watson, David Hutcheson and Jane Carr. Jane, a cabaret star of note, died in early middle-age and the others are largely forgotten today, even as 'names'. So much for fame and stardom!*

Leslie Henson was to direct the piece and it was on this production that, in addition to my other work, I was asked by Henson to be an 'assistant to the director'. Leslie Henson had been a household name during his days as star comedian at the Winter Garden Theatre in the First World War. He shared the honours there with artistes of the calibre of Dorothy Dickson, after he had leapt to fame in *Tonight's The Night*. P.G. Wodehouse and Guy Bolton had written many pieces, including the phenomenally popular *Sally*, especially for them. Later, Henson, in the twenties and thirties, was rarely out of the West End, either at the Winter Garden, the Strand or the Gaiety. Being sidekick to such an experienced and talented comedian was in itself a lesson that stood me in good stead later on, when I came to direct a number of West End comedies: *Book of the Month*, *The Impossible Years*, *Happy Holiday* and what is arguably the best of all black comedies, *The Biggest Thief In Town*. There is no greater asset for any comedian than an ability to time. Henson's own timing was supreme. I watched and made mental notes of how he showed the other established comedians how to do it. Later, I was to assist another straight play director of note, Irene Hentschel, in *Tomorrow's Eden*, a piece in which I had a leading comic part to play. This play was the brain-child of Moie Charles, Donald Sutherland and Barbara Toy. Charles and Toy later founded the Rank Film Charm School.

Whilst marking time in those first days of the war, between such engagements in straight theatre, plays with music, revues and cabaret, I played in any number of radio productions, which were big things in those days. I remember a comedy series called *The Bungalow Club*, which was written by the singer, Anona Winn, and featured the comic actor, Morris Harvey. He played a bath-chair man at the end of the pier; I was his assistant, a cheeky bloke. This was transmitted from Broadcasting House,

*Eva Bartok was in the post-war years one of the glamorous Continental stars, never out of the news. She was noted for her distinctive hats as well as for a liaison with a notable royal. Where is she today? Media publicity regarding her private life and three marriages, finally served to obscure her acting talent. But I directed her on stage and screen in several productions, and she proved better than she was given credit for being.

where I was a resident of *The Little Show*, (a late-night cabaret), which had Ivy St Helier, of *Bitter Sweet* fame and Trudi Bina, the Czech *chanteuse*, singing sweetly. Another good voice, Tessa Deane, played *The Southern Maid*, a Dalys Theatre musical comedy adapted for radio (I played the role of Lord Toshington, a silly ass). Out of town they were producing on radio, *Christopher Columbus*, a verse play by Louis MacNeice, at the BBC's Bedford studio. I played a succession of supporting roles in an all-star cast, with markedly different 'voices', to surround the Christopher Columbus of Laurence Olivier, and also went to Bangor in Wales, far from the black-outs around Broadcasting House, to play the Mickey Rooney role over the air in *Babes in Arms*, opposite Celia Lipton, who was that radio 'Babe' first created by Judy Garland.

During this period I was still on loan, through National Service, to ENSA. I became a thespian of many parts with mostly no part worth raving about, except when I occasionally toured, as in the title role of *Golden Boy*, co-starring with Pamela Brown, an actress name of the forties. This accomplished American drama by Clifford Odets was to play all the big English provincial cities, captivate the critics and leave audiences none the wiser! Later I was to direct another of the same author's works, *Rocket to the Moon*, at the St Martin's in post-war London. But in wartime Brighton I was enlisted by Baxter Somerville, owner of that town's Theatre Royal to direct a Russian play, *Squaring the Circle*, with a cast that included Mary Morris, in aid of Mrs Churchill's Aid to Russia Fund. It was all part of the war effort.

I had stayed in one wartime job after another but few posts in the forces were permanent. The tale of the 'neck' got out and I was transferred from pillar to post; that accident had made me a bad bet as a permanent stayer, even for Civil Defence, apart from the temporary office job I got when transferred to the RAF at Uxbridge. A busy war then, but its very stability was frustrating. Exercise was not encouraged and I was not in line for the Territorials, where drills were a prime necessity, especially as the war showed signs of hotting up at last. Still, I got another form of indoor work when certain pre-war skills as a director and actor were again recalled. Baxter Somerville had seen me in an American play, *Golden Boy* and out of the blue, suggested I direct

and act the leading role – quite a 'double' this – in another
American play, *Thunder Rock*, which was scheduled to play a tour
of south-coast theatres beginning at Brighton's lovely little
Theatre Royal. My leading lady in this play was Wenda Roger-
son, a player of breath-taking beauty, who was later to marry the
well-known photographer, Norman Parkinson, and unfortunately for the theatre, become one of the country's leading
models. Her stage work dwindled, I suspect because of her
inability to combine two careers. However, in the post-war
years, I gave her two 'farewells'; one when she played for me in a
revival of Pinero's *Mid-Channel* (opposite Frank Lawton), followed by the role of The Daughter in Priestley's *An Inspector
Calls*, which, in concert with *Anna Christie*, I directed and took
round the Welsh mining valleys in 1947. Wenda, alas, died
some years later, still a great beauty, her ambitions as an actress
long unfulfilled. 'Parks', her husband, survived her by a bare two
years.

Tomorrow's Eden had a cast containing a number of popular
box-office names. Diana Churchill and Barry K. Barnes headed
a star cast and I played the part of Matt, a chirpy cockney RAF
rear-gunner, who falls in love with an older woman (Freda
Jackson) by whom he is seduced. It was, to use an Air Force
expression, 'a piece of cake'. Moie Charles, was one of the
writers, who scripted the film *The Gentle Sex*, in which I also
played Taffy, a squadron leader (Leslie Howard directed). But
the film part was a 'bit', whereas the stage role was a 'chunk'.
The film was one of Howard's last engagements prior to the
tragic air accident travelling from Lisbon which cost him his life.
Leslie was an agreeable man of quality.

It was after this stint filming that I had a call to re-enlist in the
war-effort and this time it was, thankfully, with the AKS (Army
Kinematograph Service) film studios at Wembley. A variety of
work awaited me, connected with army propaganda films; at
desk, behind camera, on the film set itself and as a serviceman
actor. These, I felt, were *practical* contributions to the war effort.
Much of the work was superintended by the production manager, a chap called Lyndon Haynes. Other 'bright lights', I well

recall, were such pleasant and easy personalities as Jack Lee, Thorold Dickinson, and the seasoned Basil Wright – one of our best documentarists – and the youthful John Mortimer, long before *Rumpole of the Bailey* became a germ in his barrister mind.

Part-time National Service helped to soothe that 'neck', without curtailing my other career and I was able occasionally to accept more out of London stage engagements. One such engagement was in the revue, *Flying Colours*, starring Binnie Hale and Douglas Byng on tour; another was a musical comedy, *Susie*, with Jean Colin and Reginald Purdell, which played the London suburbs, before it folded at Wimbledon after a run of eight weeks. It was during this engagement, too, that I was, during the daytime, in the film *Pimpernel Smith*, (Leslie Howard's farewell at Denham) and *The Upturned Glass* at Riverside. In the latter, I collected a 'rave' notice, I seem to recall, from the critic Freda Bruce Lochart, writing in *The Tatler*. This was surprising, as mine was a cameo performance: I played a medical student who interrogated James Mason for what could only have lasted in screen time for some sixty seconds! An earlier meeting with Mason was during my ill-fated engagement in *Alibi*, but because of the circumstances of my fate I soon forgot all about it.

Now, the very last time of all I was to see him, just over from Hollywood, was when we found ourselves sitting together at the Old Bailey, in the City Lands, a reserved section of the Central Criminal Court. We were watching a murder trial (a *cause célèbre* of the day) in which we were both interested, known as 'The Pen Club Case'. Exchanging confidences we found that we were fellow crime addicts. However, that was one murder tale from real life that they never made into a picture. And none of the characters on trial for their lives ever got 'topped', or, as far as I know, had neck trouble of any kind afterwards!

ENSA tours throughout England were generally accomplished by coach, and through them we certainly did get around the British Isles. It was no fun for the theatrical companies who did their very best to make the chaps laugh; driving for long periods, much of the time in blacked-out areas and, after the travel, attempting to sing and tell stories. The troops, however, were starved of so much in an uncomfortable war. They put up with the tosh given them, even seeming to be, on the whole, truly grateful for what they received.

Looking back before the war, I suppose my early training as a boy actor and assistant stage-manager/understudy, both on tour and in the West End, had served me well as an apprentice for this middle stage of my life. Seasons, in variety, cabaret and musicals, gave me an all-round knowledge and free range to tackle most aspects of what is sometimes dismissively called showbiz. Certainly I was as adept in one type of entertainment as another. I had appeared in *Trocabaret*, based at the Trocadero (when my bill matter was 'Top Hat, White Tie and Tails', because this was what I wore) alongside such exceptional acts, sometimes, as Max Miller and the singer, Hildegarde.

I understudied and helped stage-manage *Cavalcade* at Drury Lane, sharing a dressing room with John Beerbohm (grandson of 'The Incomparable One') and Fay Compton's son, Tony Pelissier, who went on to become a film director. And twice I played and understudied at the London Hippodrome, when it was in all its glory; the first time in *Bow Bells* when I was also personal assistant to sketch-writer and lyricist, Dion Titheradge, and later on in *The One Girl*. My principal in the latter, Roy Royston, was, upon one occasion (a matinee performance), removed from the stage door by the tipstaff and taken to Brixton prison for a little matter of indebtedness to the Inland Revenue. Owing thousands (which Roy did), was the greatest of civil crimes in those days. Now millions are owed and invariably not repaid. Roy, a matinée idol and star of the twenties and thirties, had been married to the American heiress, Laura Gould. After their marriage broke up he continued leading the good life just as before, his debts finally catching up with him. So when his time came Roy went out, whilst I went on, literally at a moment's notice for that one matinée at the Hippodrome; I gave a 'mock up' performance so highly improvised that the plot went out of the window but the curtain stayed up (they had curtains in those days). I sang and danced and clowned and yet managed to keep within the confines of the plot (which wasn't much to write home about, anyway). I ad libbed duets with the French musical comedy star, Mireille Perry, and danced (after a fashion) numbers with the American star, Louise Brown (of *The Girl Friend* fame). There were plenty of dialogue scenes to get over with Lupino Lane and Arthur Riscoe, but as these were real 'off the cuff' performers, anyway, they saw me home, as did the chorus who backed me in song and dance while I mugged to the melody of 'Young Man of Manhattan', a fast and furious number that had initially been created by Fred Astaire on Broadway when the same show, *The One Girl*, had been titled, *Smiles*. After watching my matinée performance, Joe Sacks, the producer, hastily called a meeting of backers for a 'whip-round'. My ad-libbed performance had done the trick: that night Roy Royston was back for the evening performance!

All this varied experience in every side of theatre, since my days as a stage child in *The Windmill Man* and *Peter Pan*, helped to give me a natural nerve, as well as verve, and whether as understudy or principal, it has always been important to me to make an approach that was professional. On-stage or backstage, not least of all as stage-manager and play director, all has been executed from a professional standpoint, with a capacity for being malleable when the occasion arose. And in no branch of the theatre is professionalism more important than in play production.

Professionalism in Play Production

'We're all "professionals" 'ere' – Lew Grade, 1955

It's the co-ordination of all the elements of the drama that is the director's function in play production. The skill, understanding and imagination with which this is done will determine the effectiveness of the play, which the director must firstly interpret, by explaining the characterization, determining the emphasis, the pace, and the various intensities. Casting, scenery and special effects, such as lighting and costume, are all matters that require supervision and co-ordination. The major part of the director's work is with the cast. In guiding, regulating, suggesting, consoling, controlling and coaxing characterization from the actors, the director will hope to create that dramatic illusion required in the conception of the play by the playwright.

Such varied talents are rarely encountered by those with less than a good grounding in the theatre, those who have 'won their spurs': those who have worked and seen how the various members of the company, whether they be stage-managers, spear carriers or stars, work together as a team. The self-critical ones may finally feel themselves qualified to direct others in the professional theatre. (Incidentally, I do not believe *all* amateur actors to be automatically less talented than professional ones. Although I've always had a great respect for Max Beerbohm I don't necessarily agree with the scathing opinion of 'The Incomparable One' on the badness of the amateur actor. Many are bad, but then so are many alleged professionals.)

Professionalism is a state of mind, not always absent in the amateur, not always present in the professional. This encourages conduct, from which stem those qualities that stamp the professional: character, feeling and a methodical approach. The director, as co-ordinator, must select and confine, otherwise the written play becomes in production a messy sprawl, and this, sadly, is what happens all too frequently. If we are loud and meretricious enough, some will applaud, but that climate of liberty which we now enjoy, calls equally for a show of responsibility. In *Hamlet*, Act 3, Scene 2, the Prince's injunctions to the players, 'suit the action to the word' should be taken to heart by immature, vain and exhibitionist directors, some not devoid of talent, but lacking in taste.

The struggle for artistic freedom in the theatre has been hard fought over four centuries. It was carried on doughtily in this century by Shaw, Granville-Barker, J.T. Grein and a host of others. The only confining forces were the will of the public to accept or reject, and the official licensing machinery of the Lord Chamberlain. This last has gone, and public taste is willing to accept a degree of licence it would never have countenanced before. It is hard to remember that the hand of respectable puritanism was always alert to take the dramatist by the collar and indicate that he had gone too far, or far enough. The Lord Chamberlain banned *Ghosts* and *Blanco Posnet* in an army of others worthy of note. Shaw commented on the nature of freedom:

> Toleration and liberty have no sense or use except as toleration of opinions that are considered damnable and liberty to do what seems wrong.

Note that he does not classify opinions as those that *are* damnable, but as those *considered* so; nor is it liberty to do what *is* wrong but what *seems* so. He does not deny a law of right and wrong, but he demands the right to call it in question. The abandonment of theatre censorship throws a bigger responsibility on dramatists, actors and directors. Especially directors. Self-discipline is the name of the game.

In Chaucer, in Shakespeare, in Fielding, there is not a little earthy ribaldry which gives a healthy reaction; we are reminded of the late George Robey's 'honest vulgarity', by the torrent of learned scatology which pours out from the merry Rabelais. It is not polite to the prim but it moves to healthy belly laughter. What's wrong in that? It still remains a responsibility, carried by dramatic critic and play director, to decide what it is appropriate to stage and condone. Too many directors and critics are struggling for fame. They seem to think that they will get notoriety, become regarded as more erudite critics and more brilliant directors if they accord with those who go beyond all limits. To use our adopted catch-phrases, they must at all costs be avant-garde, to prevent being labelled passé.

If, for instance, in Strindberg's classic, *Miss Julie*, the strangling of *live* canaries is to happen on the stage, must we be prepared to see it *actually* happen? How hypothetical nowadays is such a question? The professional director should be expert enough to simulate the bird's head on the block; killing what purports to be a live canary by dint of 'production', the make-believe of writing. Imagination and creativity in acting and direction blend professional force. Audiences, transported to 'feel', cannot doubt that the 'prop' bird on the block of furniture has been alive one moment previously. To strangle deliberately a wretched live animal, as we were once threatened would be part of the action, is the amateurish way out. However, it is in the so called professional theatre that such 'happenings' are threatened. The sex act, when simulated publicly, is frequently represented as odious. To simulate is one thing, to actually master the act, fornicating in front of an audience, unless sensitively delineated with love and respect, can be brothel-fare. The audience in such cases takes on the role of the sexual voyeur.

No director of professional integrity need resort to gimmickry to get his 'effects' over. It's a sad fact that all too many directors in the theatre indulge in shock tactics as a substitute for ability and as the main reason for their names to be prominently credited in the programme. Released from the bondage of censorship, the modern theatre has shown itself prepared to explore the dark depths of man's nature, to make querulous statements about our destiny. We have also had four-letter words waved at us like banners and endless paddling in the muck by directors fishing for subjects that lend themselves to crude exploitation. With *risqué* plays, treatment counts for much; the director of quality brings both discipline and an imaginative approach to 'goings on' which, ineptly handled, underline rather than soften the obvious.

Art is an expression of life, it may be a guide to life. If artists do not, or cannot, themselves work by the light of this truth and the fundamental necessity of some sort of order, they are doing little to help an escape from the anarchy which stalks through the world with gaunt power. Only the interplay between audacity and control is capable of producing supreme artistic effects. The great dramatists – Shakespeare, Ibsen, Chekhov, Strindberg, O'Casey, Miller and O'Neill – abound in examples. A combination of such powers as understanding and service is called for in the director, too. More often than not comes audacity without control; sometimes control without audacity. Many directors are trying to express *themselves* in any shape or form that impresses by its unusualness but not by its originality, nor by a dedication to the play in hand, which should be absolute. True art – play, film, painting, music, architecture – gives an impression of the times or period in which it is created. Thus we are confronted with the difficulty of making clear 'the necessity of limitation' which in art smacks of enforced discipline but by others is now regarded as passé. I am hopeful that the decent will finally override the indecent, the naturally beautiful oust the ugly, because people occasionally have a habit of sorting the good from the bad. Unless we recognize the necessity of limitation, not only will the now defunct and dreary theatre of the 'who's for tennis' and 'French-window' school be submerged forever, but another theatre as well: the Theatre of Hope. For beauty can insist upon showing itself sometimes in the most improbable of places, in dunghill as well as idyllic surroundings.

Perhaps the time is not far distant when our children and grandchildren could be saying to their elders: 'But that's not like the *Midsummer Night's Dream* I was told about or *The Cherry Orchard* I read and grew up to expect to see when I was old enough.' It is not that the 'bare bones' aren't there, so much as the reflection fails to bear *any* similarity. There was yet another production of the *Dream* at the National in 1992 – all in mud. I've never seen such unhappy actors. All their clothes had to be washed after each performance and they were freezing as they were so wet each night. Titania had to hang upside down (as a bat!) for ten minutes. She hung by her ankles only and there was mud everywhere – both at the National and over at the costume cleaners who were, I suspect, threatening to strike! As Prospero would have had it, 'We are such stuff/As dreams are made on'. But this was nightmare rather than idyllic dream.

We shall, if we become nihilists, have got rid of the baby as well as the bath water; because without a great sweep of some cleansing force, quality theatre of the future will become merely a chamber of horrors, a medical casebook of perversion and a stomping ground for the gleeful exhibitionist of limited or no talent, but abundant impudence.

As professionals, we suffered under an amateur blue pencil in the censor's office for too long. Far from producing works of strength, quality and enlightenment, we could develop no further. Vital subjects were banned, the theatre was only tolerated as a place of escape. In order to succeed it needs drama that gives emotional satisfaction. The method used is not as important as the satisfactory result achieved. Any play that is *totally* lacking in artistry is not a work of art. Any production, when it is merely staged without an ear for sound and music, without an eye for colour grouping and general effect, is not a work of art. But when the inclusion of 'testing material' fits in with the artistic shape of a play it is quite absurd that in an open-minded society we should be prevented from seeing the widest possible range of artistic production if the directors who treat are sensitive and in earnest. Now that there is the liberty to include *any* material in *any* production, there is a need, more than anything else, for a sense of personal responsibility, maturity and, most crucially, an effective authority. More succinctly put, it boils down to self-discipline above all. With these three guiding principles they should not fail to carry audience support with them into the next century.

It has been asked, where is the theatrical avant-garde, now that it is needed? Where the innovative drama which used to be performed in small theatres (real theatres with stages to help conjure magic, not merely rooms in pubs, some the size of domestic living rooms!)? Come back, the Stage Society and those Repertory Players! From such stagings plays like *Journey's End* first saw the light of production.

For some years after the two world wars, a number of small stages were to be found in London to accommodate plays of consequence: in the twenties the Gate, the Stage Society and the little Everyman held sway; in the forties and fifties the Gate, The Torch, the Threshold, the Watergate, the New Lindsey and the New Boltons. Plays were regularly mounted, sometimes quite inexpensively. Although such venues were often small, many of them received much critical acclaim.

Today it is different. With overheads forever mounting it has become increasingly difficult for the theatre of modest pretensions. Secure financial backing for some is difficult to find, and often the venue choice is really no choice at all; a big, central London 'barn' – Her Majesty's, the New Victoria, the Dominion – or a noisy, cramped, often smelly space with no facilities in pubs and clubs. I think Jim Hiley in *The Times* (4 March 1991) sums up the current situation nicely:

> For twenty years, the term 'fringe theatre' has been routinely employed by journalists, artists and members of the public. It conjures up an image of iconoclastic talents in makeshift studios, hammering out alternatives to the mainstream fare of regional reps, commercial venues, and the two big national companies. But the present-day reality of the fringe could hardly be more different.
>
> The output of most fringe theatres has, in all but scale, become identical to that of the established companies. There are but a handful of innovative groups, their activities the least adequately funded and least reported. 'Fringe theatre' flatters the majority and demeans the minority. Once, the phrase denoted a vibrant and avant-garde. Today, it camouflages the neglect of 'research and development' in drama.

But whether you act or direct for a living, seeking the goal of professionalism is a necessity. Perhaps we should apply ourselves to marrying professional acting to professional directing, *professionally*. ('Oh, not *another* person explaining "how to act"?' I hear you say.) Surely it has already been said down the years by the masters? What about Poel and Granville-Barker in England, Brecht in Germany, Stanislavsky and all those heavy Russian books? Barrault in France and Bergman in Sweden? Yes, but perhaps it would have been better if Stanislavsky – *the* Supremo –

had been satisfied with the Moscow Arts Theatre and his dis-
ciples, and not tried to spread the message. The real artists –
Horniman in Manchester, Habima Players in Israel, The Irish
Players – would all have found their way to fame and glory, even
if Stanislavsky's revolutionary cry had never been translated
from the Russian. 'The Method' was a perfectly good sound idea
until the phonies latched on to it. Its basic intention then became
all too often a signal to improve upon the playwright in order
for director and actors to accommodate their puny individual
vanities.

Anyway, 'how to act' changes with the attitude of those in
charge. This is separate from the changes that take place from
one decade to another and from country to country. There have
been, and still are, various schools of theatre. The first kind may
still be recalled by older playgoers and theatre historians amongst
younger audiences.

The 'Actor-Manager's Theatre', much in evidence pre-1914,
was the directorless theatre. The stage-manager, then, organized
rather than directed proceedings. This kind of theatre had the
'entrance', centre back, for the star. There would always be a big
build-up for this 'star moment'. Each answered to a round of
applause when they first appeared on the stage and all the other
actors, however important to the play, were well in shadow and
facing up-stage, while He or She in full limelight, centre, delivered the text. What ho, the play! He, or She, certainly always
took solo curtains as though they *were* the play.

In the 'Commercial Theatre' productions that succeeded the
'Actor-Manager's Theatre', the stage-lights would be full-up and
the action played down-stage. 'Names' that will draw (albeit not
automatically) usually feature heavily in this kind of theatre,
regardless of whether the star, chosen at random for his or her
box-office appeal, can play the particular part for which they are
engaged. Or whether, sometimes, they can act at all, the sole
criterion being, 'are they box office?'. After all, it *is* a 'business'!
You can count the essentials for this kind of production on one
hand. There are four:

1   Play
2   Production Capital

3 Theatre
4 Actors

These are the 'musts'. 'And the last shall be first', for actors and directors are, in practice, as one.

The 'Director's Theatre' has the scenery; costume and lighting are of paramount importance, as is the director's own particular 'interpretation' of the masterpiece he all too often crucifies. *His* 'interpretation' will, of course, ensure that *he* is brought into the limelight. This theatre is the one that sometimes receives a grant from our government subsidy, under the aegis of the Arts Council. The entire country has occasionally benefited from this subsidy; although, in its operation, the ailing touring theatre has suffered a long illness, which it is managing only haltingly to shake off. The provincial product on offer is sometimes good, sometimes horrifyingly bad. And we have been inundated with 'Living Theatre', 'Theatre of Cruelty', 'Theatre of the Absurd', not forgetting 'Theatre of Show-Off', and so on, *ad nauseam*. Commercial sponsors (when not advertising on the telly) are fast becoming the order of the day. Even the newly refurbished Playhouse in the West End is compelled to acknowledge its source of sponsorship on all its programmes and advertising material. A 'soft sell' is a necessity for any enterprise of an artistic nature. All too often, the sell is hard.

From the critics of the past we can get the flavour of how so many great actors worked, Kean, Siddons, Garrick, Kemble. Closer to the present time we can read criticisms. Some of us can even remember witnessing the wondrous performances of such twentieth century luminaries as the Drews, the Barrymores, the Lunts, Laurette Taylor, and our once great and good Sybil Thorndike, to say nothing of Granville-Barker, actor and dramatist as well as producer.

The actors of the post-war period must be judged by the highest standards, as many may be writing about them in the future (if anyone is *writing* at all!); Olivier, Gielgud, Evans, Ashcroft and Guinness, yes, and Vanessa Redgrave, of course, all have been written about by their contemporaries. But will the less fashionable actor be recalled? That now dead gallery: Wolfit, Swinley, Sara Allgood, Arthur Sinclair, Maire O'Neill, Jack

MacGowran, George Elton, Martin Walker, Wilfrid Lawson . . .
The list is longer than it looks. And those of indefinable quality
today will surely be written about tomorrow – Eileen Atkins,
Juliet Stevenson, and one or two others.

Why are books about theatre not more eagerly read than those
about artists in other interpretive fields? Once, only the great
music-hall 'star' biographies and works about ballet and music
could vie in popularity with books about actors of the 'legitimate
stage' (as though the 'halls' were illegitimate!). In any event,
performers did not expect to be told how to *be* music-hall artists –
not that there are halls any longer for them to work in! (No one
knows *how* they did it, although there are basic rules which they
and 'straight' actors, have in common. They disregard these at
their peril.) The plucky and still struggling Players Theatre off
Villiers St is today the nearest we shall get to music hall and
variety. Dominic Le Foe and Alan Curtis should stand up and
bow for sitting in the 'Chair' for so long.

Perhaps a human being's curiosity about acting exists because
its very roots are only an extension of the most important game
any of us ever plays, one we play all our lives. 'Let's pretend'
fulfils one of our greatest needs. Isn't that why we want to know
about the rare actors who have lifted the playing of 'Let's pretend' into an art? Why we want to know about the comparative
few (Denholm Elliott, Robert Morley, Wilfrid Hyde White and
Rex Harrison spring to mind) who have made fabulous sums of
money 'playing the game'? I think this may be where the fascination lies, the desire to know how they did it. Not why such others,
the opposite end of the see-saw – Fred Barnes, Peter Warlock
and Tony Hancock – committed suicide; nor why George Beal-
by, Sid Field and Terry Thomas died in comparative poverty
and today are hardly remembered.

As with any other form of artistic expression, not even the
greatest actor ever achieves his goal; never finally discovers the
elusive magic secret, because the revelation never ends. As we
change and grow, so our vision of what is possible changes and
grows, and we never reach the culmination, or the destination.
Like Peter Pan, the boy who never grew up. . . .

To know what one should do, and be able to do it, are such very different matters. There are the necessities, the demands, the qualities – all must be achieved in order to realize even a fraction of what one imagines can be done. Goethe said: 'Anything you imagine you can do, you can do.' For Goethe that could be true. One thing we do know, the achievement of the aim is the least straightforward thing imaginable. We shall have to wander down a few alleys and lanes and byways, departing from the straight road of rules and regulations in order to gain the knowledge that will produce the ultimate performance. We hope, however, that in the end, our definition will have some shape and order. At least it may give rise to discussion, disagreement and consideration.

Some people want to act because they can act and feel they can. Even as small children they have this knowledge, without encouragement from elders or any understanding whatsoever about the theatre. In the same way that a child who is musical or a budding scientist or a natural dancer demonstrates a talent at an early age, so it is with some actors. These 'born' actors (sometimes surmounting enormous obstacles) almost always achieve *some sort* of success in the medium in which they excel.

It is often, though not always, most fortunate to be born into a theatrical family. These members of the acting profession (if they have inherited the magic family talent, and sometimes when they have not!) succeed, more often than not, in establishing themselves with only a fraction of the heartaches and heart-breaks which haunt the aspirant who of necessity must start from scratch.

Good looks are eagerly welcomed into show business. Their owners stand the greatest chance of making success for themselves and for their managers and agents. If these entrants are serious, ambitious and practical they will learn to act well enough to charm the not very discriminating public and often become great 'world stars'. People are hungry for the sight of that rare asset, human beauty, and will pay extravagantly to view it.

A fairly large group of children, who could have excelled in quite different and often more valuable walks of life (certainly for their own satisfaction and happiness), are guided, sometimes not too gently, into the entertainment game by ambitious parents. These are often satisfying an unfulfilled longing to 'tread the boards' themselves, or, less admirably, are aware that if success is achieved there is big money to be made.

There are those, non-workers, who could not or would not try to qualify for, or hold down, a regular job or profession. Some are attracted to the theatre and clutter it up for a few years of their lives, thinking that acting is easy. A cinch. They have the satisfaction of describing themselves as 'actors', when filling in forms, or attending at the Job Centre to collect their weekly 'stipend'; this becomes their principal skill.

That elusive thing, 'star quality', is only occasionally bestowed upon a fortunate human being who can also act and has physical magnetism. The result, then, is a Chaplin on film, a Pavlova in dance, or a Bernhardt, Duse or Irving in the theatre. Very near the top, were those Three Graces – Garbo, Dietrich and Monroe – film actresses of intangible quality, suited for screen rather than stage.

For those who get the breaks, with or without talent, but often with a lot of hard work and 'a little bit of luck', there is the large financial reward which encourages them to 'have a go'. Whatever category the applicant for a successful career in the theatre fits into, he or she should realize that in order to reach the goal he or she is striving for, the future offers work, work, and still more work, until the end. And by that we don't mean, necessarily, that he or she will always be employed! Here 'the Fringe' can sometimes, if not always, be useful. The *professional* approach is paramount whether you act or direct, whether in West End or provincial playhouses, in one night 'fit-ups', or on the platform that passes for a stage on the fringe.

Telly-Ho!

The Beeb and ITV
Four- and three-letter words

During a lengthy and varied theatrical career I found time to work occasionally in television, and in the early 1950s replied to an invitation from Michael Barry, then current head of BBC drama, to join a course he had inaugurated specifically to teach TV techniques to already established theatre directors. It was hoped that they in their turn would – on a reciprocal basis – spend part of their time, in between theatrical engagements, teaching fully-fledged technical crews how to benefit from their knowledge of actors and acting.

It was an imaginative stroke on Barry's part, chiefly due to the fact that he was, at heart, a man of the theatre, who had found himself in the wrong seat and secretly regretted having left the stage at all. He had served his theatre apprenticeship before the war as a producer, among other things, at the Greyhound Theatre, Croydon. Now, with all the ups and downs that were occurring in television with the war over, he exercised consider-able power in picking vehicles for transmission, but needed a team of competent assistants who were already experienced in *directing* actors. He had established a desk job for which he may not have been entirely fitted, temperamentally. However, with both taste and appreciation in abundance he commanded affec-tion, even if he did not always get the respect he deserved.

The classes started for the course were conducted by another technician, Royston Morley ('The Professor', as he was soon dubbed), who had written several stage plays and novels and was already technically skilled with cameras and lights from pre-war days when the telly, in its infancy, started at Alexandra Palace.

In those days, Bernard Shaw (*How He Lied to Her Husband* with Robert Harris and Vera Lennox in the leading roles) joined Thornton Wilder, Edgar Wallace and Messrs Hart and

67

Kaufman, as stage playwrights to be adapted for the new medium and were, with a vengeance! (The young Joan Miller played the leads in such TV plays by these writers as Wilder's *The Happy Journey*, Wallace's *On the Spot*, and Hart and Kaufman's *Once in a Lifetime*, at Ally Pally in the thirties.) And the few hundreds and then thousands of viewers who watched at the start of the first transmissions could scarcely have thought that the box in the corner in their suburban living rooms and parlours would in time become a domestic necessity in so many households in the land – a veritable 'One-Eyed Monster' in Allan Prior's phrase, also the title of his novel published after the war.

My fellow students at 'Morley's College', taught at Alexandra Palace (nowadays an exhibition centre), included some who later distinguished themselves in the theatre more than in TV, (Tony Richardson, for example, the first director of *Look Back in Anger*), and also Kenneth Tynan who became a household name through writing about, rather than directing in, the theatre. But of course, there were others who after taking the course, more or less 'signed on' and became for many years fully fledged staff directors, in either TV or radio, at the BBC.

I sat between Tony and Ken and all three of us made copious notes of the 'Professor''s words of advice. I developed a rudimentary knowledge of the works and finally, after some months was thought to be technically efficient enough to be entrusted with transmitted productions. Michael Barry had seen my production of the American play hit, *Come Back Little Sheba*, on the stage when it was on its run at Brighton, prior to the West End. He was now content to let me loose with actors and technicians together.

How would I master the techniques? As it was, the course had proved beneficial enough for me to be made responsible for three drama productions, all lined up one after the other – three stage plays scheduled with vastly differing styles that I'd helped adapt for the telly: *The Infinite Shoeblack* by Norman MacOwan, *The Same Sky* by Yvonne Mitchell, and *The Mask* by Tennyson Jesse and H.M. Harwood. This last named, incidentally, was a piece of Grand Guignol which the old *Daily Herald* paid the compliment of attacking in its leader column, for being too lurid! How times have changed between those fifties and now, when almost anything, perhaps *everything* goes! Still, it provided good acting roles for its two performers while creating its rumpus.

The other two, more conventional pieces which I directed in my first BBC-TV stint, were well regarded by critics and audiences alike and had, for those days, high ratings. Before commercial television these mattered less. Today the telly has become a war of the ratings.

The late Yvonne Mitchell, the actress chosen to play the leading roles in all three plays, was also the author of one of them – the first I directed after the course. In *The Same Sky* she had opposite her Ronald Howard (Leslie's son), and the other principals were Joan Miller and George Coulouris, who made a heart-rending middle-aged couple; not difficult for George who had been one of the veterans in the cast of Orson Welles's *Citizen Kane*, but more exhausting for Joan, in those days a young actress herself (and of a similar age to Yvonne, who played her daughter). For her performances in all three plays, Yvonne won the *Daily Mail* Best TV Actress of the Year Award.

Later, Joan and Yvonne were to play together again, this time in the film, *Yield to the Night*, in rather different roles, as wardresses in a prison where a character based upon the true-life Ruth Ellis (who murdered her lover and was played by Diana Dors), is awaiting execution. A few years before this film, Joan had scored a huge personal triumph in yet another piece, the stage play *A Pin to See the Peepshow*, which was based upon an execution of nearly thirty years earlier, that of Edith Thompson in the 1920s.

A newspaper TV award for handling all three productions led to my directing on television again. This time the play was Beverley Nichols's *Shadow of the Vine*, a play about an alcoholic, with Catherine Lacey and Arthur Young, two sterling actors, in the roles based upon the author's own parents. With its scenes of delirium tremens, in a tense, emotionally charged plot – an unusual mixture for Nichols – this play stirred up quite a storm at the time.

I was to produce it twice more, once for Australian television with Edward Hodge and Sophie Stewart as the 'marrieds' and then for Associated Rediffusion with Richard Bird and Joan Miller. (Interestingly, the ratings for this final production were twice those of the original!) I am inclined to think that in today's climate, with entertainment standards being what they are, chronic alcoholism – even when starkly presented – would hardly raise an eyebrow – nor would the character of the father, whose ill-treatment of his wife in one sequence leads one of the two sons (the one based upon the young Nichols), to get physically between his parents and scream at his father 'You bastard, you *bloody* bastard!!'

Believe it or not, that beer was too strong for the Beeb's TV service in the 1950s – and I received a head-office order during final rehearsals to drop the adjective 'because it is an objectionable swear-word and will undoubtedly cause offence'. However, the 'bloody' crept back in on transmission, with the highly charged emotion of the moment. It would have been tame indeed, even in those days, for such a nerve-wracked son to pour out all his protective frustration in defence of his mother with the single word 'bastard'. Today it would be the f-word. Yesterday, even 'bloody' breached the Beeb's code of conduct.

A telly series with a high rating that I incidentally suggested for the late Patrick Wymark was 'The Power Game'. This was after seeing Pat play in the 1957 Shakespeare season at Stratford (in the same company that included Joan Miller playing Constance in *King John*, Portia in *Julius Caesar* and the Queen in *Cymbeline*). It was a good season and included such actors as Peggy Ashcroft, John Gielgud, Richard Johnson, Robert Harris – and a youthful actress already charged with glorious promise that she was to fulfil fully some twenty years later, Eileen Atkins.

I had invited Pat to play the role of Sir Charles Worgan in Arnold Bennett's satire 'What the Public Wants' (a role originally played on the stage by the actor-manager Sir Charles Hawtrey in 1912). This BBC production was to be its first revival. I wondered what Bennett (who based the play upon the character of the press baron, Lord Northcliffe) would have thought about its adaptation for the new 'entertainment medium', the telly, so many years later. With its plum part for a personality of Wymark's calibre (and such stalwarts as Dulcie Gray and Hugh Burden also), I have not the slightest doubt that it was this portrayal of one of the great megalomaniacs of the newspaper world (Maxwell was to set the town alight and rob the pensioners much later), that later decided the producers of 'The Power Game' to offer the comparatively little-seen Wymark the role that made him into such a successful telly star, before his life, like others I've known, ended all too early in his career.

Apart from the various projects that were set up for the Beeb from time to time – after, as well as before, my fruitful association with ITV – there were still theatrical productions constantly cropping up for me to direct simultaneously, one of them a crazy idea by Emile Littler of making a musical version of the old stage thriller, *The Ghost Train*, and calling it *Happy Holiday*. It was the Christmas season and as Emile owned the Palace Theatre, London, at that time, what could be better, he told me, than to have such a festive piece on that famous theatre's stage with all those seasonal connotations, such as pretty schoolgirls as chorus in bouncy numbers choreographed by Felicity Gray. It was to be written by George Posford and Eric Maschwitz (original composer and lyricist of Jack Buchanan's title number in the film *Good Night Vienna*, sung by Jack to the newest British film star of the thirties, Anna Neagle). Hey presto! This pair provided many original numbers that soon had the proverbial errand boy on his bicycle whistling their tunes.

'Why me', I enquired, 'to direct such a potpourri of style and talents?'

'Because, dear boy,' replied Emile soothingly, 'I need these musical-comedy and revue types *directed*, and with your light entertainment as well as straight theatre experience, I think you're the man for the job. After all, it is a play, *The Ghost Train* set to music.'

Although doubtful, I felt gratified to receive such flattery from the Pantomime King – and when he told me the cast he had in mind to engage, with my approval, I was elated. Versatile veterans like Marie Burke, Austin Melford, Vincent Holman and Edmund Willard, mixing with Erica Yorke, Trevor Griffiths, Betty McDowall and the then popular musical comedy singer, Bernard Clifton, and Janet Brown (later Mrs Thatcher's 'double') thrown in for good luck, to help supply the love interest. With it all we had as a plus Emile's gift for 'beating the big drum', as he had shown in the past in many a 'hardy annual' London and provincial panto. Could the minuses be thrust aside?

I could resist no longer the 'Dear boy' blandishments. It was a 'musical adventure' indeed (for this was how it was to be 'promoted'), but when I saw, a few weeks later, the original play's author, poor old Arnold Ridley, sitting in the stalls during rehearsals helplessly wondering when the musical mystery of fun ended and when *his* play (upon which it was all alleged to be based) got a look-in, my heart bled.

Fortunately Arnold was able to banish the memory of this 'musical adventure' during the next two decades by going on to become one of the leading characters, (the oldest member of the Home Guard) in that long-running TV series, 'Dad's Army'. A decent man and good companion who worked in several productions of mine at The Boltons, at least he redeemed himself by his last role of all, a telly personality. He died a few years ago, having, I suspect, forgotten all the liberties taken with his beloved and, at one time, most successful play.

Emile had cast Reg Dixon, the 'Confidentially yours' comedian from the North, to play the silly-ass type of the original play script. It was incongruous casting, even in the light of the 'dog's dinner' that had been laid out for our customers' delectation. But when Reg did his 'front-cloth act' before the curtains and sang his best-known sentimental number, 'Confidentially', he brought the house down. The plot went out of the window, as in every Littler pantomime, and the house rose to the occasion. It was a pity that the box office advance that followed for the rest of the show's run didn't do likewise.

Two other productions I did for Emile in the West End, both at the Cambridge Theatre, had quite respectable runs. One he called me in to salvage, *Book of the Month*, with Judy Campbell, Hugh Williams, and Margaretta Scott heading the cast, ran over six months. The other, *The Impossible Years*, was written by Arthur Marx (Groucho's son), who asked me on the first night whether this was his play or mine. It was Emile's. It had featured, in an earlier successful Broadway production, a great Broadway and Hollywood comic, Sam Levene. For its London production, however, Emile had engaged that accomplished comedian, but very *English* actor, David Tomlinson. Although

David times like a dream, a great virtue in comedians, he simply was not typecast as a member of the garment industry of America. However, the show did its stint and nobody's reputation was much damaged, except, as was the case with the musical, the poor bloody author's.

For all my misgivings about Emile's taste I continued to think of him as one of life's great enthusiasts, a natural winner. Certainly he was a fortunate man. 'Lucky Littler', I called him in my obituary for the national press. He chose his closest associates well. The most talented of them all was his production manager, Louise Wright, whose name, Psyche, he would insist upon mispronouncing by calling her Fish. She became known as such, and merely smiled enigmatically. Unlike the majority of theatrical managers – who today will insist upon calling themselves 'producers' – I have a hunch that he really did like, and perhaps even love, in a strange quirky way, the theatre. Or was it *his* brand of show-biz, with revivals of old musical comedies, and putting 1920s thrillers to music, that he was in love with?

After a particularly concentrated glut of work with the Beeb, intermittently, and ITV more constantly, I was sent another stage-play script by Ted Willis, best known for his TV series, 'Dixon of Dock Green', 'The Huggetts' and 'Mrs Thursday'. The suggestion was that if I liked it, perhaps I might pass it across to Emile.

Ted had been a long-time admirer of what I was trying to do some years before while running my own company at Manchester's Library Theatre, and had in fact visited a number of my productions upon behalf of the old *Daily Worker* for which he was, in the late forties, drama critic. It was not unusual for his fellow London critics on the nationals – W.A. Darlington of the *Daily Telegraph* was one; Alan Dent, then writing for the *News Chronicle*, another – to review new productions during my season there, and Willis was, I recall, loud in his praise for a number of them, including Arthur Laurents' play *Home of the Brave*, a striking study of anti-Semitism in the American military forces of that time. This production was also seen by the one-armed impresario, Peter Daubeny, who promptly went and purchased it behind my back as a vehicle for the youthful Richard Attenborough. Retitled *The Way Back*, and with eccentric casting and limp production at the Westminster Theatre, London, it was not the success that *Home of the Brave* had been in Manchester. When I saw that my name had been credited on the programme as associate producer I protested and asked to have it removed. The final curtain fell on the piece before they were able to do this and I did not see Dickie Attenborough again until he and *The Mousetrap* entered my life together.

I read the Willis play, *Hot Summer Night*, liked it (with reservations) and in due course passed it across to Littler, who was bound to spot its potentialities for the West End stage and media spin-offs, when it showed the love interest between a young white girl and black boy who actually kissed on-stage! This was not a normal occurrence in 1958, but I was determined that any production I directed should be truthful and not 'sexsationalized'. Willis had written a thoughtful play in line with his trio of serious and hugely successful TV plays that I had directed already on television: 'Woman in a Dressing Gown', 'Look in Any Window' and 'The Young and the Guilty'. His motive now in making a socially conscious play, *Hot Summer Night*, entertaining but not meretricious was to be applauded, and I endeavoured conscientiously to curb Emile's showbiz-like propensities in advertising and publicity to the best of my ability.

Racial prejudice runs right through the play as a recurring theme, and keeping this in mind was, for director as well as writer, imperative to the production as a whole. It was no pioneering job – other colour-bar plays, *Deep Are the Roots*, *Anna Lucasta* and *Raisin in the Sun* had preceded it on the West End stage. Nevertheless, it was honest and superbly acted by, amongst others, Joan Miller, John Slater, Andrée Melly, Harold Scott and Joyce Howard. The latter was returning to the theatre after a long spell as a leading film actress who had at one time played Juliet while still in her early teens. Harold Scott was a much neglected actor of many parts who served the theatre well, but when he grew past it, and the sole acting triumph of his shaky career – playing the leading role in Ibsen's *The Wild Duck* in the West End – was largely forgotten, he was content with bits and pieces in telly series of one sort and another. When he died

(*top left*)
'The Guv'nor' in Napoleonic stance
(*top right*)
Our mother as a girl before her children
were born
(*left*)
The author impersonating Vesta Tilley,
at the age of 5

The four Boulting boys with
Winnie Jones ('Nannie')

The Boulting family at home in Hove in the 1920s: *left to right* Peter, John, Roy,
Guy, Rose and Arthur

When they were married in 1948 Joan was starring in *Dark Summer* at the St Martin's Theatre and Peter was directing Donald Wolfit in Ibsen's *The Master Builder*

Donald Wolfit and Rosalind Iden as Solness and Hilda in Ibsen's *The Master Builder*, directed by Peter Cotes at the Westminster Theatre
(*photo Russell Sedgwick*)

Joan Miller and Wilfrid Lawson in Joseph Losey's stage production of *The Wooden Dish* at the Phoenix Theatre, 1954 (*photo K. Hutton, for Picture Post*)

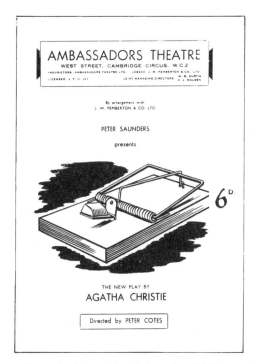

AMBASSADORS THEATRE

WEST STREET, CAMBRIDGE CIRCUS, W.C.2

PROPRIETORS: AMBASSADORS THEATRE LTD.   LESSEE: J. W. PEMBERTON & CO. LTD

LICENSEE: J. F. H. JAY   JOINT MANAGING DIRECTORS   W. G. CURTIS
H. J. WALDEN

By arrangement with
J. W. PEMBERTON & CO. LTD.

PETER SAUNDERS

presents

6 D.

THE NEW PLAY BY
AGATHA CHRISTIE

Directed by PETER COTES

Programme from the first night of *that* play, 25 November 1952

Joan Miller in Anouilh's *Medea* at the Oxford Playhouse, 1957 (*photo Kenny Parker*)

Joan Miller as Portia and Alec Clunes as Brutus in *Julius Caesar*, Stratford-upon-Avon, 1957 season (*photo Angus McBean*)

Julie Andrews and Andrew Cruickshank in *Mountain Fire* (*photograph Armstrong-Jones*)

Flora Robson, Joan Miller and
Joyce Carey in *The Old Ladies*, the
author's 1969 revival of Rodney
Ackland's classic drama from the
1930s

Joan Miller as Queen Constance
in *King John*, Stratford-upon-Avon,
1957 season (*photo Angus McBean*)

Joan Miller and Roger Moore in *A Pin to See the Peepshow*, based on the Thompson/Bywaters case. This was Roger Moore's first important role (*photo Eileen Darby*)

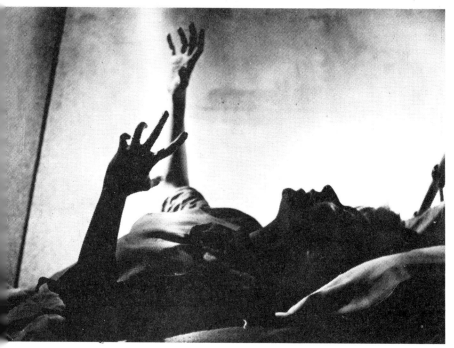

'A great, if harrowing, performance by Joan Miller in *A Pin to See the Peepshow*. . . . (*New York Times*). Julia Almond spends her last night in the condemned cell (*photo Eileen Darby*)

Joan Miller and Peter Cotes, partners in and out of the theatre

Joan, as she was for so long
(*photo Armstrong-Jones*)

over a score of years ago, the *Daily Mail* headed its short obituary notice of him, seven lines in all, with 'Dixon of Dock Green Actor Dies', as though a fine character-actor's career could be measured by his final appearances in a small role in a long-running pot-boiler. (I had once shared a dressing room with Scott during the run of a Jack Waller musical extravaganza, *Hearts Are Trumps*, a piece starring Hermione Baddeley, Alfred Drayton, Wylie Watson, David Hutcheson and Jane Carr, which, with a production by Leslie Henson, was better than its title.)

Hot Summer Night did quite well as a specialized play in the West End at the New Theatre (now the Albery), until it exhausted its audiences. It had been well received by the critics as a play and was afterwards made into a film with a cast of names who, it was thought, might be more acceptable to cinema-goers. However, it failed to repeat its stage triumph, collected a poor press and proved more meretricious than artistic. Had the original hand-picked cast remained intact for the film, *Hot Summer Night* might have become an arts-cinema cult film. As it was, it died quickly, if painlessly, with only Emile and Ted making any profit out of the film rights.

The following year a volume of television plays by Ted Willis was published under the title *Woman in a Dressing Gown and two other plays for Television* (Barrie and Rockliff, 1959). It was dedicated by the author, 'To Joan and Peter. They were produced by Peter Cotes, and Joan Miller created the leading roles in *Woman in a Dressing Gown* and *Look in Any Window*. This book is dedicated to them in affection and gratitude'. A third play in the volume, *The Young and the Guilty*, was also brought to the small screen by me, and later, in view of the success of that production, I also directed it at Elstree as a feature-length film with several members of the original television cast, including Campbell Singer and Andrew Ray, together with such actors as Phyllis Calvert, Edward Chapman and the ill-fated Janet Munro (who got a long screen contract on the strength of her performance as the teenage heroine but died tragically young).* The film critics

*Janet made her last appearance in a leading role in my stage production of Lesley Storm's comedy, *Look No Hands*, which played at the Fortune Theatre over a dozen years later. Both Munro and Storm died shortly after the run closed, making a sad ending to a funny farce.

unanimously praised this comparatively small-budget film and when it was shown subsequently at the Warner Theatre, Leicester Square, in a double-feature programme, it quickly won star-billing after being hailed as a sleeper. Since then the film has had a number of repeat showings on television.

Never in television history has there been a more volatile and colourful character than the BBC's Huw Wheldon. Down the years, in and out of telly, he was constantly cropping up in my life and crowned his enthusiasm for our long friendship by publicly acknowledging the Beeb's indebtedness for my bringing them all sewn-up the TV rights in P.G. Wodehouse (but more of that later). The last time we met, not too long before he died, Huw was deputizing most ably for Alistair Cooke at the RSA, and making what was a characteristically 'Huw Wheldon speech' while delivering a paper on TV, PR and broadcasting, all in one. He mastered them all.

I had known the BBC's 'sunshine boy' (arguably its foremost producer and entrepreneur) for many years. He had originated 'Horizon' and 'Monitor' among other adult programmes, and his engagement of such talents as Ken Russell to direct 'Elgar' (which Huw produced) set new styles and standards that were to remain long in the memory.

We met initially when, following war service, he was the sole representative of the Arts Council of Great Britain based in Cardiff, and I was embarking upon my tours of the Welsh coalfields with *Anna Christie* and *An Inspector Calls* in 1947, it was Huw who left his Cardiff office (which he manned single-handed) and appointed himself to run me around the coalfields – a different miners' venue or hall each night – in his little Austin 7. He was even then a most conscientious chauffeur and no touring director could have wished for a more congenial, witty and caring companion than Huw was in those early days – and ever after.

Later he took his chance in television, leaving the Arts Council to become the leader he was cut out to be, and commanding both respect and great affection. (He'd inspired such feelings during the war, which had ended for him with honours, unwounded and in a command in the Royal Welsh Fusiliers.)

Later still, when in television myself, we met again. Huw ruled as a top-brass practitioner for over twenty-five years at the Beeb, encouraging such men as Humphrey Burton, Ken Russell, Norman Swallow (incomparable as editor and director alike) and John Schlesinger, a group that can be trotted out as examples of this flair in fostering and appreciating talent.

Huw had a distinct style himself in presenting his miniature masterpieces. A heavily explicit delivery was deliberate, his characteristic way of reminding audiences of his personal literary favourites. And his gifts as an interviewer, as well as a presenter, would have put those who came later – the Wogans, Parkinsons and Aspels – in the shade. It was fortunate for many, in what was to become a field of the personality cult, that they never had to compete with one who was a 'natural' and would easily have outclassed every man-jack of them.

But going public and putting his stamp upon arts programmes at a certain time was only one of Huw's accomplishments. A veritable Mister Punch to look at, he was tall, dark, lithe and very Welsh-sounding. He brought fresh air, an infectious laugh and novel thinking into the stuffy offices and austere boardrooms of Lime Grove and Television Centre, as well as the studios themselves.

Becoming Controller of Programmes, as well as Director of the Service, Huw was a trouble-shooter who reorganized so much in the Beeb that had been constipated until he, drawing on his prowess as a performer and his executive experience (via the Arts Council), set out to let the world know that the standards established by Kenneth Adam, who preceded him as Controller, would, if anything, now become better. He had his inevitable detractors ('Huw Wellbred' they called him) and his fans. He was much admired by TV's best critic, Peter Black, while Philip Purser, another critic, was to sound Wheldon's trumpet epitaph when he wrote:

He was a tireless speaker at conferences and seminars; he visited every European broadcasting organisation and descended on America, carrying the word that the British had a God-given monopoly in telling good stories on television. He was the last of the big spenders in every sense.

But he was much more than that, as I learned from personal experience later. As a chief in charge of all executives' work, at a crucial period in his glorious career (and at the same time as he was producing such TV programmes as 'Portraits of Power', 'Men in Battle' and 'Sketchbook'), he virtually demanded in his office that I dismiss an actor from the cast of a play I had produced on a Sunday night before a repeat transmission went out on the following Thursday. All plays went out live in those days. The actor in question, a known drunk, was indispensable to the play and, although he had slurred his words on the Sunday (a natural manner of speaking for him), I resisted Huw's coaxing, pleas and even threats to get an alternative artist and rehearse him, at full pressure, between the Monday and Thursday. Huw's wheedling climaxed with a raised voice that became more 'Welsh' than ever as he ordered me to sack the culprit, there and then. I refused. The actor in question was, despite everything, one of our finest, and his sacking at this late juncture would have been unthinkable. Finally, the furious onslaught subsided and Huw went to his office window for a pause that seemed never ending; silence, while he looked down at the White City traffic passing in the distance for what must have been two minutes but felt like two hours, before he suddenly wheeled round on me and with an uproarious laugh, his face wreathed in an expansive smile said, 'You're about as ruthless as I am!' We both smiled hopelessly, the tension broken; the actor was saved, my director's prerogative to make the final decision was honoured, and the play's second transmission turned out to be an unalloyed success.

A letter from that formidable 'legend', Grace Wyndham Goldie, was delivered to me personally by hand in the producer's box of the studio after the performance. 'Grace', as she was only called behind her back (for she was a 'power' in the Beeb at the time) was in raptures. She loved it. I keep her letter to this day because it marked a signal triumph for the actor concerned, as well as the production as a whole. Things might have been quite different if I had succumbed to the outwardly fiery, but finally gentle, Huw's blandishments of only four days earlier. I read it aloud to the cast to seal the issue as the technicians were dismantling the set. It had been a turbulent production first time around but a triumph on its second transmission. 'Which just goes to show', as the late Robb Wilton had it. . . .

Leaving my BBC-TV apprenticeship long behind me, I was appointed in 1955 to head ITV's first drama department as senior producer and director. These were the formative years when the larger-than-life Controller of Programmes for the new company, Associated Rediffusion, was an Englishman, Roland Gillett. He had gone to learn the job some years earlier in American TV, where he had produced the 'I Love Lucy' (Lucille Ball) series and had come back bursting at the seams with ideas for the new British TV organization he had been asked to head. 'Bill' Gillett, as he was known had a galvanizing way of inspiring others. And yet when the history of ITV is ever referred to nowadays, nearly forty years after its launch, his (unlike Wheldon's at the BBC) is the one name nearly always overlooked in the list of those constantly trotted out in anniversary tributes. As one who worked closely with this tall, gangling, Alistair Cooke look-alike, with the blue eyes, fair hair and infectious laugh (and American accent superimposed over his natural, straight English one) I find this exclusion curious, to say the least. As a character and a talent he deserves to be recalled. Certainly without the galvanizing energy and ability of this one man in those early days of chaos, muddle and confusion, Channel 9, as it later became known, might well have been unable to open until very much later.

Bill Gillett's contribution was unique, and 'battleship' or no 'battleship', as the sailors connected with the vast enterprise liked to call it, no one else possessed his expertise in this commercial minefield. It was Bill's flair alone for creating a team, at both Stratton House off Piccadilly, and Kingsway's Television House later on, which saw that ship to port at the outset.

Bill's charm, easy manner and loyalty to those with whom he worked, marked him out from the rest. And he was always ready to admit his mistakes and 'carry the can' for those who served under him – a rarity in this respect among telly executives. Orson Welles was one of the big mistakes he had to admit. He had commissioned a series from Orson, who went on editing it until long after the scheduled date for completion and never actually delivered the goods. For months after Orson's enforced retirement from this project, miles of footage were found, long uncut, in various machines. An expensive mistake.

Admittedly, the first Controller of Programmes left hurriedly, quietly and supposedly under a cloud over one weekend, when the building was deserted and most of the 'skeleton' staff that got the show on the road subsequently, were out of London, or away for the long weekend. However, there is no reason why a blanket of silence should still be dropped on one man's notable achievement in getting independent television on the air on the scheduled date.

It was part of my job as Senior Drama Producer, to direct the first series of commercial TV films, which were made at Shepperton Studios. I made a dozen or so of the first twenty-five films, each lasting an hour, under the umbrella title 'London Playhouse Television'. Superintending the work of others and appointing the directors of the films that followed were parts of the job. All were made under feature-film conditions, and I had competent and enthusiastic film crews working on every production, and a number of actors from the screen and stage of marked ability were in such pieces as *The Macropolus Secret*, *The Offence*, *Winter in Ischia*, *The Hungry God*, *Woman in a Dressing Gown*, *The Haven*, *Two Letters*, *Tigress on the Hearth* and others. Robert Harris, David Markham, Mai Zetterling, Felix Aylmer, Hugh Sinclair, Eva Bartok, Eric Dodson, Hugh Manning, Hugh Burden, Maximilian Schell, Ralph Michael, Phyllis Calvert, Yvonne Furneaux, Nora Nicholson, Basil Sydney, John Franklyn-Robbins, Campbell Singer, Mary Merrall, Jane Eccles and Edward Chapman, were but a few of the talented artistes who peopled the various casts; among many who went on to become film stars were some getting their first chance. (I recall the almost unknown Sean Connery and Robert Shaw as two small-time crooks, in the prologue of the telly adaptation of the Edgar Wallace play, *The Terror*, when it was made for the 'box' at Shepperton. And Catherine Boyle, too, who played a bit role of 'the other woman' in St John Ervine's fine play *Jane Clegg*, with Joan Miller as Jane opposite Jack May, and Alfie Bass, Mary Merrall and Henry Oscar playing other leading roles.)

Yes, there were stars and aspiring stars in that series; all of them marked by an ability to act well and *inside* each of their characters when called upon to do so. As a group we kept together whenever possible.

One's work on TV Playhouse was greatly thwarted at the beginning by an industrial dispute between the business boys at Stratton House and the film union, the ACTT. In order to be a producer or director and walk on the floor, one had to be a member of the trade union as well as one of the executives of the company which was making the film. I was in both camps and constantly being called upon by Management and Union to take sides. This, while I had my personal viewpoint about the internecine warfare, was very difficult. I was in the middle of the crossfire, and my duty lay both with the company, who had engaged me as a key executive, and with the union, to whom I naturally, also, had loyalty to serve as a member to the best of my ability. The work we were producing would have gone ahead more smoothly if there had been a professional management at the top, but these were nice, often inexperienced chaps, jolly Jack tars who came from the emerging new business world, rather than the world of theatre, film or television.

Settled finally, the dispute created a bad feeling which was never completely dispelled.

We managed to take time out from our numerous engagements in the sixties as both actress and director by doing a play on Broadway titled *Hidden Stranger*. Joan starred opposite the Hollywood film actor, Torin Thatcher, and I directed. However, although the piece had a fair run at Broadway's Longacre Theatre, our opening and the whole of the first week of the run clashed with a newspaper strike, in consequence of which none of the critics on such important papers as the *New York Times* and *New York Herald Tribune* covered the première. The only method of arts coverage, then, was the newscaster, and radio and TV commentators who were sport and crime reporters ordinarily. So fewer theatre-goers than would have been the case otherwise heard that we were on, until word-of-mouth carried the day and the major critics attended later.

The piece itself was not bad in parts, and was well played on the whole. As in other American productions with British stars, there was an American supporting cast and this one contained the redoubtable American character-actor, Fred Tozeare (well known as a leading man in many American TV crime series) and Michael Lewis, son of the famous American novelist, Sinclair Lewis, and his wife the political journalist and war-reporter, Dorothy Thompson. It was a happy cast but a disappointing run in a city so dependent as New Yorkers are in being told that it was *on*. Those who listened to the various radio and TV reviews were not part of Fun City's average audience. And the word of mouth, though good, wasn't good enough to ensure a long run.

Joan returned to play the lead (opposite Stanley Holloway and Herbert Lom) in a film at Elstree, *No Trees in the Street*, while I started a film which had script trouble and was nearly abandoned before it was scheduled to begin, *Bitter Harvest*. It was a bitter experience from every angle and the sole solace for a short time was that we were both working in film studios as a change from the relentless grind of television which, unless one can take the periodic leave from its tentacles, can be overwhelmingly frustrating in the long run.

We soon managed to take time out from working in England when, after periods of concentrated work in both the film studio and theatre, we were offered a joint contract to travel to Australia. This turned out to be a fruitful engagement and we found, despite the then low standard of Australian television, that inaugurating a drama department and output in Melbourne's Channel 7 was the type of pioneering work natural to our dispositions and talents.

We attempted to bring – and I like to think we did help bring, from what happened after our departure – a radical change in the fare meted out as punishment to some viewers who wanted relief from the monotonous diet of panel games and done-to-death American serials and series. It was a diet that proved indigestible to thoughtful viewers, and for the rest it was a long-suffering endurance test of the sort the earlier TV viewer in England had absorbed *before* the war. There was a steady exposure of such personalities as the local favourite, Graham Kennedy, with his boy-next-door, stock-in-trade gift-of-the-gab, and it must be said, a more professional host in Gerald Lyons, who became a local celebrity through his interviewing of media personalities as they passed through Melbourne on their way to such other centres as Sydney, Perth and Adelaide – where yet more local channels were to be found. In later years many of those who worked with me at Channel 7 found themselves, as locals (producers, writers, technicians, actors), being given chances which they took and made good.

But our visit was long before many good films had started coming out from Down Under, and such a notable achievement as the film *Picnic at Hanging Rock* was a dream still unrealized. Indeed, when we were there the only channel of consequence transmitting at the time was ABC TV, the government station, and I watched it with some interest while still busily stockpiling films for TV during our defined limited engagement. Channel 7 was to be networked throughout that vast land and three of the plays I directed (*Candida, Long Distance* and *Suspect*, with Joan playing widely contrasting roles in all of them) proved a welcome change from those episodes from the dregs of the American TV market.

Looking back I like to think that the English exports played some not entirely negligible part in introducing higher standards to crews and artistes who were only too willing to cooperate and often hungry to learn. None of the pieces – all of them stage plays I'd adapted for the small screen – proved too highbrow for the majority of viewers. And as for the reaction of the press to our visit, our intrusion into the native telly scene proved manna from heaven. A staple diet of professionalism was a change from the 'mechanical crap we are fed all the time for the most part – inadequately acted, indifferently directed and primitively photographed', as one TV critic put it in his column. In other words, we two pommies were welcomed by press and public alike with open arms and chorus of praise.

Since then there's a brand new Australian movie and TV industry born out of the ashes of its former self and standing comparison with the output from other countries throughout the world. Nowadays, it's not only their wines that are for export but often their TV and film productions as well.

We returned to England refreshed from our labours and glad to have worked among so many friendly folk. We left behind many warm hearts, and knew that the radical alterations in hours, working conditions, exercised through the testing of local talent, as well as producing four full-length feature films for cinemas and television, had done nothing but good for the locals and left us satisfied with the overall journey we'd made for so many months past. That output had been backed by an initially resistant *Melbourne Herald* which had financially interested itself in TV and had brought the two Brits over to impart their know-how to the locals. They finally had the satisfaction of getting the whole of our output sponsored by the powerful General Motors Co. and it was their name that presented the 'Hour' attached to *their* product.

Upon returning to London, I received a cable from the Snowy Mountains Authority organization, based in Cooma between New South Wales and Victoria, asking me to direct a documentary film dealing with the 'opening up' of that part of Australia by the famous Count Strezlecki, a Polish aristocrat who had left his native Poland for Australia at the turn of the century. The vast project in which British Petroleum had invested ratified the offer and I was contracted to research, write and direct a film that was finally shown to selected audiences world-wide as a soft-sell plug for BP under the title of *When Men and Mountains Meet*.

Being based for some months in the Snowys, a district high up from its surrounding cities of hundreds of miles distant, gave me a feel for the country and its people that lingers to this day, and although I have never been back Down Under since, there is a corner of it firmly secured in happy memory. In the Snowys are all the countries and colours in the universe, and living in Cooma and travelling out to our sites for shooting, I was made to feel an honorary Australian. And few things can be nicer than that.

If certain plays, such as those by Agatha Christie, J.M. Barrie and Tennyson Jesse – all highly contrasting – have played major roles in my theatrical career as actor and director, there are many others (some of them listed under 'Career' in the Appendices of this book) to which I have become greatly attached. There were also some fictional characters which television was able to exploit on occasion, rather better than the theatre had done down the years, for example: Bertie Wooster and Jeeves.

My lifelong admiration for P.G. Wodehouse made me proud to help in transferring those two comic immortals from the printed page to television for the first time in their history.

It was in 1966, with ITV behind me and live theatre work to come, that I presented what subsequently became a record-breaking series on BBC, 'The World of Wooster' starring Ian Carmichael and Dennis Price as Bertie and Jeeves, respectively. My designation as associate producer on the credits was no mere sinecure.

Many television interests, both in England and abroad, had been trying to secure the coveted rights to adapt Bertie, Jeeves and all that wonderful gallery of comic characters for many years. I was lucky enough to be able to negotiate directly with the author himself and perhaps help him to see how his special creations could be successfully transferred to the small screen.

A meeting was arranged by my friend, Peter Watt, the literary agent, between hopeful producer and the author. I took off for the US, my ultimate destination being Remsenberg, Long Island, where 'Plum' Wodehouse and his wife, Ethel, lived. Arriving, I outlined for them both the plans I had made for the characters' future if once they were entrusted into my care. After several lengthy talks over a long weekend, and elated by an obvious interest and warm hospitality, I returned to England no more than cautiously optimistic that my negotiations had succeeded. But soon, Peter was on the phone with the news that I had been granted an option, 'with permission to televise Jeeves and Wooster' in what were to be (*in my opinion*) the best possible circumstances to introduce them to an even wider public.

The BBC, being made aware of this catch (for such news travels fast), and unsuccessful themselves in their efforts to persuade the elderly author to let them televise such a series, sounded initial negotiations with me. However, certain contractual conditions promised to Plum needed to be fulfilled before I was satisfied. I kept both author and agent up to date during every stage of the interminable discussions which then started in earnest. In the end it took nearly six months before a contract was concluded to general satisfaction. And then Mills (director) and Wearing (adaptor) were true to the spirit of Wodehouse in both thinking and execution.

Casting had gone ahead slowly but when we had our Bertie, the Jeeves and the rest duly followed and the adaptation of the famous stories for the small screen was completed. When screened later in the year, to the plaudits of public and press, the celebrated author wrote to me, indicating his awareness of the correct casting of the principal characters and expressing satisfaction with the result of the first episodes, flown to his home by the BBC. He signed off a highly congratulatory letter with 'Thanks again to my onlie true begetter'.

From one series emerged another, and great was the rejoicing that a great humorist in the last years of his life had helped make so many extra millions world-wide laugh. Ethel died soon after Plum's own departure and, calamitously for me, our mutual friend and agent, Peter Watt, also died suddenly at about the same time. Shattering! Like lightning, advances were made from other quarters for the rights to the rest of the canon. With no Watt to safeguard them, my exclusive rights passed into other eager hands. Today, Stephen Fry and Hugh Laurie, both expert, play the roles on ITV that were first created, some thought memorably, by Ian Carmichael and Dennis Price.

And so today as I write, in the autumn of 1992, my visit to Wodehouse, nearly thirty years ago, continues to bear fruit and flourish. And that great comic writer of unique English characters continues to be heard on BBC radio from time to time through the loving adaptations of his lifelong admirer, Richard Usborne, he who is truly without doubt, Plum's 'onlie true begetter'. . . . He it is, who with the late Guy Bolton, Plum's stage collaborator and perhaps his oldest friend, has kept Wodehouse's name and reputation alive in fair winds and foul – and it was to him I sent Plum's final letter to me – a worthy finale to a good and trusted business association that also became a friendship. I felt that nobody deserved to possess this precious letter more than Usborne, whose copious writings on the master occupy a special place on the bookshelves of all Wodehousians and now grin down upon me as I write. . . .

The meeting with Wodehouse and his wife was a 'red-letter' weekend for me. One of those occasions that I shall not easily forget, only perhaps comparable with an unexpected 'journey' I undertook twenty years earlier with our present Queen's grandmother, Queen Mary, in 1946. Her Majesty was visiting my own little theatre, the New Lindsey, to see a special matinée performance in a club theatre of a banned play I had directed, *Pick-Up Girl*. The elderly former monarch had expressed a desire to receive the principals of the production, (Joan Miller, Ernest Jay, Jessica Spencer and David Markham) backstage in the bar of the small club theatre at the end of the performance. In the royal party, apart from the Queen's lady-in-waiting, Lady Cynthia Colville, were the Earl and Countess of Athlone (Princess Alice). The entourage separated and were shown the steep steps it would be necessary to navigate, there being no lift. Defying protocol, I presented myself as the one (manager as well as producer) who would perhaps be best to escort Queen Mary, while others of her party went ahead.

It turned out to be a lengthy journey under primitive conditions, with Queen Mary valiantly climbing but stopping upon every other step. I did my best to take her left arm, the right was clutching a bannister attached to the wall. Every few moments the regal personage would halt for a few seconds to gain her breath and engage in chat regarding the theatre in general and, in particular, the entertainment she had just witnessed. She had been absorbed by it. It was a play much ahead of its time, dealing with the then taboo subjects of juvenile sex, venereal disease and child-abuse. It contained, in the course of the two and a half hours the Queen had just sat through, many four-letter words; she had desired to see the play without cuts. Despite what must have been a physical ordeal for her (a journey to a long play clearly taken against the advice of members of the royal household and the Lord Chamberlain, the Earl of Clarendon, who in his capacity as Theatre Censor had banned the play from public performance) she remained outwardly unruffled, upright as a ramrod, if more than slightly out of breath as she reached the top – and highly complimentary about both play and performance. The artistes, eventually presented to her were far less composed after playing their strenuous roles, than Queen

Mary herself. A formidable figure from afar, she unbent when close to, and inquired of Joan Miller after the formal curtsey had been made: 'Is the next play by Somerset Maugham also?'!!

An avid playgoer (with limited theatrical knowledge, perhaps), Queen Elizabeth II's 'grannie' nevertheless made up in enthusiasm what she lacked in other directions. Certainly her surprise visit to a struggling little theatre, prompted by the play's theme of juvenile delinquency, served to overturn an act of censorship which had precluded the transfer of the play from a small theatre in Notting Hill Gate to the wilds of commercial Piccadilly Circus. In the West End it played to capacity audiences in two of its largest theatres, the Prince of Wales and the Casino (now the Prince Edward).

Hannen Swaffer, the most flamboyant journalist of that day, wrote of the royal visit in the columns of the old *Daily Herald*, and ended his account with the opinion that the elderly Queen's only motive in visiting the play was that her eldest son, subsequently Duke of Windsor, had himself been a juvenile delinquent, and that her presence had been encourage by her visit to an East End juvenile court, where her friend and lady-in-waiting, Lady Cynthia Colville, was Chairman of the Bench of Magistrates.

In recent years our royal family have come to be less highly regarded than they were in the past, even though Queen Elizabeth II has long sought to uphold those family values so long maintained by her grandmother and mother alike. Certainly Queen Mary, when on the throne, although admired and respected by the majority of her subjects, struck awe into many people due to her commanding presence, rigidly regal and supposedly puritanical outlook. It was my exalted task that day, long ago, to shoulder the honourable burden of the still heavy, though gaunt and rock-like monarch who, as with the other sovereign ladies to follow her, daughter-in-law and granddaughter alike, proved to be a 'professional' to her fingertips.

No Run

Waiting For Gordon

As an actor in the West End my career alternated between long and short runs. *Cavalcade* was one which seemed to go on for ever at Drury Lane, while such others as *Caravan* at the Queen's, with a much more star-studded cast (headed by the most popular leading actor of his day, Cedric Hardwicke, at the Queen's, Shaftesbury Avenue) and *The Last Stone* at the Phoenix (in which, glory be to God, I had my first and last West End taste of *acting* stardom along with Czech beauty, Mira Reymonova, and John Slater as co-stars) were 'off' within a few weeks of opening.

As a director, I have seen similar instances, with the longest running of all West End plays to offset a one-night-stand on Broadway. There were others, also – long'uns and short'uns – and even once upon a time a tale of skulduggery (not only aboard a pirate ship) that, in one year, never opened at all. 'Its name, dear children', as Barrie's heroine, Wendy, might have said, 'was Peter Pan'.

As a child and then teenage actor, I appeared in *Peter Pan*, playing, over many different years on tour and in the West End, the parts of John, Slightly and Starkie. The play was in its glory then, the twenties, thirties and forties – the title role being depicted from its beginning by actresses of such distinction as Nina Boucicault, Gladys Cooper, Edna Best, Madge Titheradge, Zena Dare, Fay Compton, Pauline Chase and Jean Forbes Robertson (conceivably the best of the lot). In the thirties, the latter was the actress most associated with the role, 'keeping the pirate ship afloat', as it were, long before *Peter Pan* became a vehicle for film or pop stars.

It has been pointed out by the critic, Kenneth Hurren, in his book *Theatre Inside Out* that 'There are a number of children's plays, some based on TV series, others on well loved books, which do well, but there are others that survive only one or two Christmas seasons of a few weeks.' Hurren goes on to list such evergreen favourites as *Toad of Toad Hall, Treasure Island, Alice in*

Wonderland and *Winnie the Pooh*. He omits to mention that hardy perennial by Frederick Bowyer, *The Windmill Man*. As a child in the twenties and thirties I got to know and love this play, mainly through appearing in it as Major-General Tabloid, at the Victoria Palace. Jointly with *Where the Rainbow Ends* it 'represented' the Italia Conti Stage School in the West End. At that time, the twenties and thirties, Conti's was the leading school of dramatic training for the stage. It could count to its credit such ultimately successful artists as Gertrude Lawrence, Anton Dolin, Noël Coward, Roy Royston and many others. I was in *The Windmill Man* (as the fiery little Major-General Tabloid), when my contemporary and dressing-room pal was Jack Hawkins, he who was later to adorn many successful plays and films as a star player, died tragically in his middle age while still in his heyday. Other fellow students of mine were Billy Speechley, who left the theatre despite what looked like a promising career, and Brian Glennie who disappeared after playing Puck in Basil Dean's *The Dream* at Drury Lane.

The discerning Kenneth Hurren went on to observe that 'It is not until such shows become really established and can make use of the same sets and costumes year after year that they become really profitable investments. None of course has anything near the record of longevity achieved by *Peter Pan*.' (Alas, the tense is in the past now, in these not so gay nineties, and we should alter it to 'had'; Barrie's dear old play, first produced in 1904 at the Duke of York's theatre in the West End, no longer has a regular London production.)

Peter Pan has had a long, eventful life for many reasons. Any vandal can make a bad play out of a masterpiece; it's a sad fact that if any director decides to stage a play back-to-front no one will stop him. Whatever may have been done to it, and whatever its detractors may say, *Peter Pan* is an acknowledged classic that has succeeded in running, albeit not consecutively, for many more years than even *The Mousetrap*. This success is rare despite the fact that in its history it has suffered the criticism of being labelled, amongst other things, 'fey', 'old-fashioned', 'unhealthy', 'sentimental', 'embarrassing' and, perhaps worst of all at the box office, 'intellectual'.

It also proved a magnet for over sixty years to those who

delight in devising ever more incongruous ways of producing it. Like a TV panel game, it's a childishly simple exercise, awesomely attractive to those who seek fame without ability.

The late W.A. Darlington of the *Daily Telegraph* saw the play in his first years as a critic, and again many times in following years. He described one particularly vulgar post-war revival as, 'A fine jewel in a tarnished setting'.

He could easily have been referring to another production I remember (but would be best forgot), in 1980. An article appeared in *The Times*, in the form of a pre-publicity interview with that year's Peter who was at pains to point out how unlikely it was for the *present* production to survive another season (my italics). The interviewer seemed to have hoped, rather optimistically, for a return to 'first principles' and a magical new production, based upon Boucicault's original. The article continued that any new production should have love and respect for the play; and a jealous regard for its status as a masterpiece that is timeless in its appeal to audiences of all ages.

As it is, its profits serve to benefit that worthy cause, the Great Ormond Street Hospital for Sick Children, and even seasoned drama critics might therefore feel intimidated, being tempted to water down their professional opinions. No excuses however, could be made for most of the 'jazzed-up' versions seen in the 1980s. They succeeded in vulgarizing a unique offering, a masterpiece that contains a blend of fantasy and wisdom in equal measure. In fact, for the sake of its author's memory, I was bound to ask myself during the intervals, how much longer could the play's reputation withstand the witless onslaught of such productions? Why was there this apparent refusal to stop fooling about with what is nowadays called 'the story line'? One that belongs to that rare bird, a fragrant little story that has made the transformation from literature into theatrical folklore.

For every person who has seen the play, there must be countless thousands who have known down the years the meaning of 'The Boy Who Wouldn't Grow Up'. This symbol Barrie never found necessary to describe, except through the mouth of Peter Pan, when he crowed, 'I'm Youth, I'm Joy, I'm a little bird that's broken out of the egg!' while a mystified Hook stops his duelling and shouts back, 'Pan, who and what art thou?' and then, continuing the fight, 'Oh well, to it again' as he raises his sword in a further attempt to slay this creature whom he, like all the other Hooks in the world, will never understand. It is the everlasting contest that appeals so well to so many. Eternal Boy against Pirate Chief. They represent a whole lifetime to a parent watching the play and a daily playground battle to a child. They speak to us all.

For many years before the demise of a regular production I attended revivals of my favourite play. Throwing off dull care and setting out optimistically I would say to myself that surely *this* time it wouldn't be as bad as it was last time, that it couldn't be. But it could be. Each time in the last dozen years of its life, I've come away from whichever big theatre was housing this theatrical delicacy feeling more depressed than ever.

The sub-title, *The Boy Who Wouldn't Grow Up*, was often cut (a not unimportant point, in itself) and the absence of John Crook's marvellously melodious score also seemed a major error. The music of *Peter Pan* is an integral part of the whole. It's as necessary to Barrie as Sullivan to Gilbert and as Tenniel to Lewis Carroll. Apart from being so much a part of that whole, when used, it fits – exactly.

There had been several really ghastly productions in the sixties and this was the position when the late Roger Lancelyn Green (acknowledged authority on the play and author of several books about the piece, including *Fifty Years of Peter Pan*) went on record by stating:

> The future of the play would be safest in the hands of Peter Cotes. He is quite clearly the ideal man to produce it, the only man as far as I know who has the expertise combined with the necessary knowledge and love of the play.

Perhaps I may add without immodesty that a number of others who know the work shared Lancelyn Green's view. This enthusiasm for *Peter Pan* dated from my own experiences in it, as I have already mentioned. Additionally, I was by this time an experienced West End director with a number of classics to my credit and my own production company. So I was asked, was I an active applicant for the contract when the lease for its production was 'up for grabs' in the early seventies? Would I put my money where my mouth was? Indeed I could and would; that much had been urged upon me at an early date in the negotiations, when I had written formally to the Great Ormond Street Hospital, where a Mr Gordon Piller was designated an Honorary Agent for Peter Pan.

This letter to Mr Piller was dated 10 November 1970 and there were further meetings between us in the following weeks, once at my office and several at my club. Prior to these meetings, however, I received a visit from a Mr Cyril Hicks, whom I had known some years previously as being associated with the office of Bernard (now Lord) Delfont. Hicks, I afterwards learned, had been asked by Piller to sound out my detailed proposition. Hicks, incidentally, was also present at the subsequent meetings between Piller and myself. It was to become significant later that he was now acting as a liaison man, representing other parties rather than my own. Tom Arnold Presentations was one of these, presided over by Helen Arnold, widow of the theatre, circus and ice-show impresario. Tom Arnold Presentations had had one previous connection with *Peter Pan*: they had presented it on ice at The Empire Pool, Wembley for the 62–63 season.

Curiously, there were no protests, and I soon had the impression that a close and friendly relationship existed between Piller and the Tom Arnold Presentations office at the London Pavilion. A meeting was arranged between myself and Gerald Palmer (Mrs Arnold's director of productions). Palmer suggested that Tom Arnold Presentations act with me in my application for the play and offered to put at my disposal extra capital and such costumes as were appropriate from those that had been used in the ice production. They also suggested that they would arrange, through the provincial theatres they were associated with, the six-week tour that would follow a London season of the play. I cautiously agreed to a co-production on the understanding that I would direct.

This was heady stuff, and thus encouraged by such a source, and knowing that the play was coming shortly into the public domain, I threw my hat into the ring as one of the bidders for the rights in what was, I thought, virtually an open field.

By now I had also made certain of my financial backing. Private bankers were not slow in coming forward to guarantee the cost of obtaining the rights of such a coveted property (and afterwards helped launch productions in the West End and provinces.)

Hence this formal application for the *Peter Pan* production rights. I stated in my letters that I would stage the production in the 'first class manner' that I had understood the Hospital Trustees to expect from anyone who was favoured as a suitable producer. The adrenalin flowed and I began negotiating for a six-week matinée season at the London Coliseum, suggesting more generous royalty terms than Great Ormond Street Hospital had specified with any commercial managements. At no time, either then or later, did I think of offering any bribe to any individual.

The sequence of events from that point is curious, especially with regard to the availability of the London Coliseum which was then, as now, the home of the English National Opera. The Managing Director at that time was the late Stephen Arlen. We met to discuss the matter in early February. I found Arlen highly receptive to the idea of my directing, but nevertheless, he wrote (February 25th) that he was 'a bit perturbed' by the technical aspect, i.e., flying wires in the afternoons when there had to be evenings of opera and, 'When we finally go into it all, it may not be practical, on such a restricted basis,. to launch *Peter Pan* at the Coliseum at all.' In the light of Arlen's judgement it hardly seemed possible to take literally a gossip column item that appeared later in the same week disclosing that Mrs Helen Arnold was buying the stage rights to *Peter Pan*, planning to present it at the Coliseum next Christmas. Incidentally, the disposition of the rights was not to be decided by the Hospital Governors until June, and it was still only February.

I consulted my solicitors after receiving a letter from Arlen on March 23rd to say that he had written to Mrs Arnold to refute her facts, and sending me a copy of what seemed to be a reprimand:

I have been having informal discussions with Peter Cotes on the subject. That a statement should appear in print is, to all intents and purposes, unsatisfactory and discourteous, as

it clearly means that we have to organise ourselves with a
very simple operatic repertoire, and this we must know at
least twelve months ahead.

A few days later yet another news item appeared, this time in
the *Daily Express.*

Peter Pan will be staged in modern dress in a £40,000 charity
production at the London Coliseum this Christmas, the
Great Ormond Street Hospital for Sick Children said last
night.

The press was putting out a version different from my understanding. Their information was more or less correct, that others
were to put on the play at the Coliseum. Whereas I was being
told it was unlikely in various letters and statements. In fact the
Press Association put out the original statements which were
picked up by the national press. The full text of their story
referred to Tom Arnold Presentations as applicants for the *Peter
Pan* rights, in no way connected with me and at no time, either
then or later, did they suggest an arrangement for me to direct, despite another news items released in the *Evening Standard*: 'Tom Arnold
Presentations will do the production and Peter Cotes will direct.
    Because of the discrepancy between the published news and
the information in Arlen's letter to me, I wrote to Arlen yet again
at the end of March seeking enlightening, while Goodman,
Derrick and Co, wrote likewise to Piller. Arlen ignored my letter,
but Piller replied to the solicitors: 'The Hospital Governors are
making a final decision about *Peter Pan* at their Board meeting at
the end of this month and we shall be in touch with you then.'
March came and went, but nothing further happened until May
26th when Arlen himself was quoted by the *Daily Telegraph* as
now forecasting a Christmas season for *Peter Pan* at the Coliseum. In reply to my bewildered query, referring of course to his
meeting with me in February over lunch, and to correspondence,
especially his letter of March 23rd, Arlen replied on June 2nd:

Thank you for your letter. Really, the never ending
confusions about *Peter Pan* are impossible. I would request

you to get on to the hospital and discuss the whole matter
with them I can have no further part in it. I am merely
trying to negotiate *Peter Pan* next Christmas for the
Coliseum, with the people who were originally associated
with you, on the understanding that they had a contract. It
is not for me to involve myself further.

If only because of the last sentence and because there could
hardly have been any greater confusions than that occasioned by
his own conflicting statements, this is surely an extraordinary
letter, the reply of someone who is lacking in frankness and
under considerable pressures of one kind or another. It may even
seem to the dispassionate observer that on this point the dirty
tricks were evident. Though by whom, for whom, and with
whom, can only be conjecture. Not that I now wondered much
further, being involved in another production at the same time
and making plans for the next production after that. However
my naïve reluctance to accept that an individual has no chance
against the big battalions in such a matter (and doubtless also
because the managerial cut of a likely £30,000 per year – a big
sum in those days – too high to be discarded by anyone) drove
me on to the bitter end.

The end had, of course, been reached unofficially, behind my
back; its full impact was yet to become apparent to me. I had
had several more conversations with Lord Goodman over the
matter, although it was being dealt with by others in his firm.
But upon receipt of Arlen's last letter (2nd July) I wrote yet
again reminding them of our previous conversations, and of a
phone call Arnold Goodman had had. They reassured me that
Mrs Helen Arnold would produce *Peter Pan* only over Lord
Goodman's dead body. Admittedly *I* was by that time far from
well! However, Arnold Goodman, to whom I personally
appealed, promised me that he would now have a word with
Stephen Arlen.

I was advised further to write to the Chairman of the Hospital
Board, Mrs Audrey Callaghan (wife of the then Prime Minister,
James Callaghan). Mrs Callaghan, no doubt rightly, declined to
see me on the grounds that she had not seen any of the other
applicants for the contract. She wrote, interestingly, that since

the Board's knowledge of theatrical affairs was not great, they had decided 'to seek professional advice, which I believe to be of the highest order to assess the applications'. The date of Mrs Callaghan's letter was June 21st; she did not indicate that any decision had been reached at that time, although it should be recalled that as early as February of that year Mrs Arnold was making statements to the press saying that she had obtained the contract and would present the play at the Coliseum.

On June 29th, a letter from the House Governor of the Hospital, Mr P.W. Dixon, informed me that 'a contract has now been engrossed between my board and a major theatrical controller for the production of *Peter Pan* on the English stage for the next seven years'. A later letter from Dixon on July 12th stated that 'on Wednesday of this week we shall be holding a press conference to break the news that the stage rights are to be awarded to Tom Arnold Presentations'. And so they were.

Looking back on this tale of falsehood, perfidy and double dealing, one is forced to the conclusion that *Peter Pan* was now being made so expansive and expensive that only a really enormous theatre (apart from the Coliseum) such as the London Palladium, could house it. Certainly, during the seven years' licence given to Tom Arnold Presentations, pop stars such as Lulu essayed the much coveted dramatic title role. Also, TV personalities from 'Dallas' had a shot at it.

The net result was that at the end of the day the Hospital Governors found that they had given the property to a company that in the sixth year of the seven-year contract, could not mount any London production at all.

It is not unusual, in the commercial theatre, for a scheduled production to be dropped when it becomes clear that it is not to be profitable. Few can have imagined that *Peter Pan* in London at Christmas would ever fall into that unhappy category, least of all, apparently, the Governors of Great Ormond Street Hospital for Sick Children. (See Appendix 2)

Short Run

On the one day of the year . . .

On 13 April 1951 the following news item appeared in the pages of the old London *News Chronicle* under the bold heading *Cotes v. Lord Chamberlain*:

> Peter Cotes is once more to take up the cudgels in his battle with the Lord Chamberlain's office when on May 8th he produces at the New Boltons Theatre Tennyson Jesse's play *A Pin to See the Peepshow*, based on the Thompson-Bywaters case.
>
> He prepared this play for production at the Manchester Library Theatre a year ago, but was informed that the Lord Chamberlain had refused a licence for public performance, although Frank Vosper's play dealing with the same subject was allowed West End production.
>
> . . . now he is to try again and the Lord Chamberlain will be invited to see his Tennyson Jesse play during its three week season at the Boltons.

But that wasn't how it all began. Years earlier, in the late forties I had tried unsuccessfully to stage the play in my own theatre in Manchester, prior to London production. When the piece was in full rehearsal, with a cast of twenty two professional actors already engaged, (headed by Joan Miller and Tony Britton) the Lord Chamberlain said belatedly that no licence could be granted. This British censor had been sent the script some weeks before the play went into production, and I, somewhat understandably, mistook the silence that then prevailed, to go ahead. That the production must be called off, as a brother of a character in the action had made a last minute intervention to the Lord Chamberlain, was quite a blow.

Later came two further clashes with the Lord Chamberlain's blue pencil (which had long taken unto itself the dictatorial right of making 'suggestions'), over *A Pin to See the Peepshow*. The Lord Chamberlain's 'suggestions' had to be accepted, or banning of the entire play would follow, however serious and thoughtful it might be. There was never any hope of reprieve. The long struggle against the censor in the British theatre is a tortuous one and in the last decades Bernard Shaw, Ibsen, Strindberg, Harley Granville Barker, amongst many other writers of note, have felt the censor's interference. In the post-war years, the tyranny was gradually being relaxed, until in the 1960s theatre censorship was abolished. This was not the early sixties, however, it was the fifties, and at the time I only saw one chance of getting around the ban (it was *never* to be removed in this country), and that was to acquire my own little club theatre, The Boltons, which I quickly re-christened The New Boltons.

It was in the early fifties and at the New Boltons theatre that what had become known as the Thompson-Bywaters Case of thirty years previously, was to be staged in a dramatization by two distinguished writers. The verdict of many thousands of people since that double execution day in January 1923, is that Edith Thompson should not have been hanged. The Bywaters-Thompson case has always been a talking-point in favour of ending capital punishment, especially for women. It has been featured in numerous books, from formal accounts of the trial to fictional re-creations, the most famous perhaps being F. Tennyson Jesse's bestseller *A Pin to See the Peepshow*. The M.P. Beverley Baxter quoted the case in an emotional plea against hanging in the House of Commons Debate on capital punishment: ' . . . Edith Thompson had disintegrated as a human creature on her way to the gallows, and yet somehow they had to get her there.' Apparently two warders from Holloway contacted him to say he must use his influence to see that, 'Never again must a woman be hanged'. The last wardress to see Edith Thompson alive gave me much unofficial 'help' at the rehearsals of the play. She guaranteed the authenticity of the procedure in the condemned cell.

By the early 1950s Tennyson Jesse's playwright husband, H.M. Harwood, had adapted *A Pin to See the Peepshow* into a play, which was again blocked by the Lord Chamberlain. When, however, I presented it at The New Boltons theatre *club* in 1951, it ran for eight weeks longer than it had been scheduled. Many senior members of the government went to see it and left full of praise. The catchy title referred to Leo (alias Bywaters) and

Julia (alias Edith) recollecting their school days when he charged her a pin to see his 'peepshow', a shoebox affair full of little toys and things, with pink paper pasted over a hole through which one peeped. The production had an extraordinary impact on the audience, largely due to Joan Miller's *tour de force* in the star role. The reviews, from all over the world, were never ending, despite no public performances of the play in Britain and only a very brief run in New York due to under-capitalization. To quote from only two reviews will give an idea of Joan's skill in re-creating the character inspired by Edith Thompson.

> Miss Joan Miller's performance of the murderess; volatile, vulgar; incurably romantic, and at last terrified into insensibility, is an astonishing achievement. It will be long talked of and no one should miss it.
> Harold Hobson in the *Sunday Times*, 20 May 1951

> This is a play and a performance that those who see will talk of for years.
> *Variety*, 7 July 1951

Not only did the play through its central performance stir up the capital punishment controversy all over again, but it also provided the comparatively minor interest of many prominent people rushing to see a 'banned' play because of its relevance to a subject of national importance. No one will ever know how much *A Pin to See the Peepshow* helped to influence the British Government's decision to abolish capital punishment in 1965.

Then it went to Broadway with Joan Miller again as Julia. Roger Moore had a shot at recounting the 'happening' in *Plays and Players*, long before he became a world star. (See Appendix 3)

> To anyone except the 20-odd people like myself who were concerned in the production, *A Pin to See the Peepshow* must seem to have been the biggest flop of all Times Square. And the people who had seen the play produced in London at the Bolton's Theatre and knew that only the interference of the Lord Chamberlain prevented its transferring into the West End must have felt there was a story behind the fiasco.
> There was a story – one of the craziest in the crazy world of the theatre. . . . We opened 'cold' (without the usual provincial tour) at the Playhouse Theatre, New York, on

September 17th, after three well-received public dress-rehearsals. It was a tremendously successful first night, and we were told in our dressing-rooms afterwards by enthusiastic people who had seen the show, including Hermione Gingold and Oscar Hammerstein, that we had a sure hit. . . . Now the New York critics are notoriously trenchant. . . . But there was not a disapproving note. The play, the production and the players were praised most generously. Joan Miller's own performance was hailed in such terms that *A Pin to See the Peepshow* might have been expected to run on the strength of that alone.

So I spent a lazy, blissfully happy day, arriving at the theatre in the evening expecting to find an excited company congratulating one another on their success. They were certainly excited, but not in the way I had imagined. For on the notice board was pinned a brief, fatal, note to the effect that the play had closed.

The misfortune for us however, led to world stardom for Roger. At that sole performance, executives from MGM were in the audience and impressed enough to offer the clean cut young Englishman a film contract. It was the period when new young male faces were being spotted. For the rest of us it was a bloody funeral and a monumental disappointment.

So what went wrong? I discovered later that many had stayed away from seeing the play at its only Broadway performance because it was held on Yom Kippur, *The* High Holy Day in the Jewish calendar. Seventy-five per cent of the theatre-going public on Broadway is Jewish, and those not orthodox enough to be in synagogue would stay away so as not to be seen enjoying themselves on this special day.

Neither the actors, nor the director, could have foreseen that our buoyant, enthusiastic 'shoestring' producer (who had set up the Broadway showing on the strength of witnessing the play in England) would have no capital after the first night to keep the show running. She had gambled on sufficient advance bookings in ticket sales for the play to pay its way at the beginning of the run. Brooks Atkinson (then the doyen of New York drama critics) had written enthusiastically enough about Joan's performance alone to merit the expensive taking of advertisements.

This general publicity could have been used most effectively to exploit the play's potential. The good notices for the leading actress alone, should have been on the marquee of the theatre – the 48th St Playhouse, one of Broadway's most prestigious theatres – for all to see. Joan's performance in the play was electrifying, witnessed by Kenneth Tynan's letter on seeing her in London. (See Appendix 4)

> Kenneth P. Tynan
> 19 Upper Berkeley Street, W.1.
> 10th June 1951

Dear Miss Miller,

. . .No performance in my memory has broken down so many of the barriers that hide the last deepest wrath of the human heart. . . . My wife and I, normally a gay enough pair of cynics, cried in the taxi home . . . we had seen the clearest most amazing piece of acting in London and we both knew we would never have the courage to see it again.

I should be grateful if you could find a moment to tell your husband what a delight I took in his production – especially in the party scene (scene two) and the magnificently clumsy, casual and cold blooded handling of the last scene of all.

In every generation there are about half a dozen actresses who are always better than their script: and actresses like this deserve, need plays to be written for them. Their skills demand vehicles. For me, at this moment, you are one of these; and eliminating perhaps some of the over florid and pompous gush in this letter, I intend to hang on to that opinion for at least twenty years.

> Again, many thanks:
> Yours sincerely
> Ken Tynan

Well, twenty years later Kenneth Tynan was to have blossomed into one of this country's most powerful drama critics. His influence grew while his range was extended through writing for the *Observer* and the *Evening Standard* over here, and later for the *New Yorker* in the States. Not one word was heard from him, however, when he became dramaturgist for the National Theatre under Olivier's banner. We waited the 'call' for Joan that never arrived. This was odd to say the least, especially taking into account that in the intervening twenty years Tynan, in his official capacity as critic, had seen Joan many times and had, despite his caustic reputation towards certain star actresses, consistently praised her. On several occasions he had been positively ecstatic (in particular with two American plays, *The Man* and *Come Back Little Sheba*) if not 'carried away', as he clearly was after witnessing Joan's performance in *A Pin to See the Peepshow*. I remained baffled: What went wrong?

A sequel to that weird experience, that Short Run, proved to be equally odd. In 1987 a biography of the now film star Roger Moore, by the critic Paul Donovan, led to a libel action in the Law Courts. Moore's ex-wife, the singer Dorothy Squires who had first introduced Roger to me, sued the publishers W.H. Allen, together with Donovan for libel. Her action stated that they had defamed her in the course of the biography and cited a section of the work that happened to be an interview that Donovan had had with me.

I agreed to be called as an 'expert witness' – that one who had certainly given her ex-husband, out of a job and seeking work in New York at the time when I was casting *A Pin to See the Peepshow*, the engagement that led to this subsequent film career and world stardom. I had been unequivocally admiring of her efforts in trying to secure the engagement – it was, I told the judge, as much due to her doggedness in the first instance, as to anything else, that Roger Moore landed the role with me. Not having known or seen Miss Squires on the stage or concert platform previously, I had formed the opinion that she must be an agent, since she did all the talking while Roger remained silent at the first interviews. And I admired her tenacity at that time in selling the idea that her unknown 'client' should at least be given the chance of auditioning for me.

Clearly, it was only upon much later reflection, with the collapse of the marriage, that Miss Squires's decision to sue, an action in which I was not joined with publisher and author, led her to view me in a different light. In the witness box I found to my surprise that I was to be subjected to a hectoring cross examination by the plaintiff herself, who had decided to conduct her own case as counsel for the prosecution! She now seemed to think that I had been in some way uncomplimentary about her in the course of the interview with the biographer. At first astonished, I became genuinely more saddened than exasperated by her tactics (seeing a sole person taking on the big battalions is usually a sight that commands my sympathy). For some obscure reason she appeared determined to put me on the defensive, but although goaded, I refused to display anger in the witness box, for I felt more pity than anything else for one who was determined to treat me more as an adversary than anything else when I was under fire. Pity, perhaps, and even a bit of humour emerged out of the proceedings which were ultimately to prove so expensive for this modern Portia. I suspect that right up until the judgment was read, she relished her current role of singer-turned-counsel. The judge must have thought likewise, for in his judgment he was to find a satisfying feature of a prolonged cross-examination to be my evidence, when he said:

> I was deeply impressed by the manner in which Mr Cotes
> delivered his evidence in a forceful cross examination. I have
> no doubt that whenever the evidence clashed, I preferred his
> to hers. In fact the evidence given by Peter Cotes was
> wholly reliable.

Apart from those words, which spoke for themselves, it was a bittersweet ending to my association with an ill-fated play, albeit one that had provided a wonderful part for my late wife, an actress who had made it unforgettable through her performances in London and New York. Its authors didn't forget: when they died the play was willed to me and was produced by BBC TV as a four-part serial during the eighties, with Francesca Annis in the central role. (I was not consulted as to casting having sold my television interest outright. If I had been, I should have chosen Eileen Atkins for the part of Julia (Edith Thompson), but as it was Miss Annis played it very well indeed.)

The ownership rights continue to bring me in occasional royalties from provincial stage productions, but these are less numerous than perhaps they should be owing to unusual difficulties in finding suitable actresses for the leading role. Meanwhile, I have kept my distance from active participation in staging that strange, exciting, but ill-fated tale of injustice, both on-stage and off.

Long Run

'Three Blind Mice, See how they run . . .'

Her (Christie's) dialogue does not bear any resemblance to
what one says in normal life. She always seems to have a
great deal of repetition. For the actors to make these repeti-
tions sound viable is very difficult. I reckon if you can play
in an Agatha Christie play, you can play in anything. I
think that everyone at drama school should be made to do
an Agatha Christie play. If they can make it real, make it
sincere, then it works 100%, let's face it, but if they can't, it
is better to give it up. It's a real test for anyone.

Mary Law, actress, 1976

It was early 1952, The phone bell rang . . . Richard Attenborough was on the line. He had already made a success as a
juvenile character-actor and film star in such hits as *Brighton Rock*
and *The Guinea Pig*; many of these films he had made for my
film-producing brothers. Dickie, as he was generally called, had
seen quite a few of my stage productions in the past. Up until
now we had never worked together, although before his screen
career he had been an actor in the theatre. He wanted me to
direct a new Agatha Christie mystery thriller, *Three Blind Mice*, in
which he was to make a starring return to the stage opposite his
actress wife, Sheila Sim. Sheila had only recently been appearing
as an *ingénue* in my try-out production of William Inge's play
Come Back Little Sheba, the first London production of that American drama success.

I had first met Dickie Attenborough through my brother John,
who had given the young stage actor his first break in films. He
had spotted an unusual quality in the juvenile, one that was to be
carefully exploited by John and Roy in numerous films that were
to set the seal on Dickie's career. This early professional association between my family and the Attenboroughs was brought
about when Dickie was tested by John, for a part in a propaganda film, made by the RAF, called *Journey Together*. John was

113

at this time a flight lieutenant, and Dickie an A/C 2. Edward G. Robinson had come across from the States to star in this allied effort, and the youngish Attenborough, with very few films to his credit tested successfully. A long string of features followed in the post-war years. With the Boultings back as civilians, Attenborough was seen under their banner in such film hits as *Brothers in Law*, *Private's Progress*, *Carlton-Browne* and *I'm All Right Jack*. He became one of their contract players. Our association had, therefore, a good foundation on which to build.

I must confess that I was only half interested in Dickie's proposition at that moment, because among a number of other things I was getting *The Biggest Thief in Town* transferred from the Duchess to another London theatre. This play was to become known as the first black comedy. It was a mixture of wit and uproarious laughter that was followed in succeeding months and years by such hilarious examples of the genre as *Entertaining Mr Sloane*, *Loot*, *The Killing of Sister George*, *The Birthday Party* and *The Caretaker*, to name but a very few of the glut of off-beat and sometimes tasteless pieces following, that were soon filling West End stages. The trappings of death, smiles, pomp and tears made them, when astutely concocted, entertainment that was less than sad, and sometimes very comic. *The Thief*, however, had needed careful direction and a sense of humour to make it the success it became. (See Appendix 5) I think having me to direct him might have been one of Dickie's stipulations before embarking upon his return to the stage. He had not always been well looked after by theatre directors in the past.

Apparently a few days before Dickie's phone call to me there had been a lunch between him and my brother John. Dickie's film contract with John fortunately contained a release clause which enabled him to appear in an occasional stage play, if the right one came along. John agreed to release him for this new Agatha Christie piece. Dickie's phone call on that spring morning was to let me know that a meeting might be arranged between Peter Saunders (his new managerial associate, currently running another Christie play, *The Hollow* in the West End) and myself. Saunders, he assured me, would put me 'in the picture' and was writing to me, and he, Dickie, very much hoped that a new play by Agatha Christie would be enough to my liking to agree to direct it. After an exchange of letters between Saunders and me, a meeting was arranged. (See Appendix 6)

The play was called *Three Blind Mice*, and had been adapted by its author from a short radio play of that name. It ran only half an hour, but was now to be enlarged to normal theatre-length. The radio play had initially been written as a tribute to Queen Mary for her Eightieth Birthday Festival Programme. I listened to Saunders over lunch at the gracious Carlton Hotel in the Haymarket (unlike *The Mousetrap*, now dead and gone). When he mentioned the elderly Queen, I recalled her visit, on the eve of her Seventy-ninth birthday, to my own little theatre. The Queen had come to see my production of *Pick-Up Girl*, that historic play about juvenile delinquency (a subject that interested the Queen greatly, according to her lady-in-waiting, Lady Cynthia Colville, upon whose suggestion Queen Mary had expressed a wish to see it). Lady Cynthia was a good friend to my little theatre. She was Chairman of the Bench of Magistrates at the Toynbee Hall Juvenile Court, and having been present at the play's first performance, she was so fired by it that she entreated Queen Mary to let her arrange, upon her behalf, a command performance. Looking back I think it was this serendipitous connection with the Queen that decided my attitude about whether or not I should direct *The Mousetrap*, as *Three Blind Mice* came to be called. I went to our home in Kensington to read again the script Peter Saunders had already sent me with his first letter. It was plain to see from a less cursory glance that a good job had been done in adapting the thirty-minute radio play into a three-act stage play, a fact confirmed when I settled down to read it even more carefully that evening.

Apart from its more obvious thriller-killer atmospheric qualities, I could see its potential with the right cast of talented players, headed by Attenborough and Sheila Sim. Dickie had attempted to explain these qualities to me before I was conversant with the whole play. He was of the opinion that the piece must benefit from my handling of it, and in his expansive way reminded me that it would be of benefit 'for you darling also'. There can be few people more persuasive than this lovable, gnome-like character when they want something, and I think I may say, without undue immodesty, Dickie wanted me. He had seen my productions of *Come Back Little Sheba* and *Home of the Brave* a short while earlier (his wife Sheila Sim, had played a prominent role in the former), and was astute enough to know that *The Mousetrap* required the correct treatment. It was a mixture of comedy and drama, and a director was needed who would be aware of where pauses could create a powerful silence and where exact timing would cause an equally powerful belly laugh. Moreover, the piece needed pace, rhythm, tension and verve, all of which Attenborough had observed in certain of my other productions. And as my brother, John, was to observe later, 'Dickie's mad keen on having you direct him, as he thinks only you can do it'. Certainly, as a director, I had a number of successful comedies and thrillers to my credit already.

Following further talks with both Dickie and Peter Saunders, an arrangement was made for my agent to be called into the negotiations. I could see the piece not merely as a vehicle for a star performer, but as a medium for a director with a rather special talent of infusing tension into a production. It was clearly a matter of some urgency for Dickie because of contractual film obligations, and Saunders seemed most anxious to settle his director. It had to be the *right* director for the piece, one who would be contracted without delay to ensure his participation in the casting, which in any event, had been scheduled to take place shortly. The majority of the cast, when finally chosen, had worked with me in the past, and expressed themselves as looking forward to working with me again. Among others I suggested who were ultimately cast in the original production were Jessica Spencer (my original 'Pick-Up Girl'), Aubrey Dexter (the police sergeant interrogator in *A Pin to See the Peepshow*), John Paul (an actor I had already directed in BBC TV's thriller *The Mask*) and, of course, Sheila Sim (Mrs Attenborough) in *Come Back Little Sheba*. I have always enjoyed working with artists in a team that I have worked with before.

After a further series of studious readings I still had certain reservations about the script itself. At the outset I made a number of suggestions whereby the play's structure might be improved, and its underlying, as well as overlying, potentialities could be more thoroughly exploited. These reservations were in the first instance discussed with Dickie and Peter Saunders.

Later I put these ideas to Agatha Christie herself, over meals which she hospitably provided at her flat in Chelsea. She listened most carefully to all my suggestions on several occasions and finally confided that now she saw the play very much as I did. Throughout our meetings and story conferences I found her to be always most co-operative.

There are those connected with the theatre who have criticized Agatha Christie as a negative character when she was away from the theatre or her other work. I am bound to say that in my experience she was the soul of equanimity; throughout our association in study, dining-room, theatre and rehearsal room, not one hard word was ever heard between us. She was protective of her 'brain child' as all good mothers should be, but only up to a point. Her shrewd side was uppermost in her mind when constructive decisions had to be made about removing or adding a line or even a speech here and there. She would grasp an idea to strengthen the play or even alter characterization wholeheartedly.

Various chroniclers of the 'personality cult' have found her, as a person, a trifle heavy and even disagreeable. Looking back over the passage of many years, I remember Agatha Christie rather differently. I have a distinct impression of a not unfriendly country house maiden-aunt type – the sorts of characters often in light comedies, with deceptively jolly looks, who, despite their sometimes capacious physiques, possess firm, no-nonsense hard cores, and in the last act usually triumph over topsy-turvy adversity to the delight of their audiences. This sort of person is sparing with her words too, with a dislike of non-essentials, and Agatha in her detailed letters to me, some of many pages, as well as her scores of postcards, showed a similar dislike. She wished at all times to relieve herself of spare talk and theatrical chitter-chatter. She refused to obscure the main issue by the side-tracking digression that all too often passes in the world of the theatre for constructive discussion. What she did possess was professionalism; a willingness to co-operate once she had made her mind up, as well as a degree of receptivity not always to be found in highly successful writers when their 'brain child' is being transferred from the page to the stage.

Indeed, her reply to my written request that the prologue of

Three Blind Mice should be completely cut before the curtain rose on its first night, was prompt and unequivocal. I felt that the dialogue here between the characters was tedious, and held up the progress of the play. The replacement, conceived between author and director, was played in semi-darkness with various sound effects such as police whistles, footsteps, and shouts. This appeared to me to create the correct atmosphere for the play that followed. The mime prologue would be set in a London street, where a murder is being committed. Agatha replied by letter: 'I think this is an excellent idea. When you and Dickie have decided exactly how you want the play to open, it can be re-written . . .' Then follow two tightly typed, single-spaced quarto sheets of counter-suggestions, of extra cuts and possible dialogue to be inserted at certain spots. Six replies, most of them detailed, to my six suggested changes. The least detailed is on the fourth point where, after being asked by me to give the play a little extra dialogue on one of Dickie's exits, she replies simply, 'Agreed'. A mistress of non-essentials, indeed. She must remain in the mind of the director of her most successful play a passive woman at home, and the thorough 'pro' at work.

As to my old chum, Dickie, now Sir Richard Attenborough, film producer and director, he must always remain a role-model for the man who holds the playing cards close to his chest. Apart from being enthusiastic about our working together before and during *The Mousetrap* (and ecstatic about my direction of the play itself), he has never since expressed any other reason why he urged me to direct 'the little thriller' (as its author called it) in the first place. But whatever the drift in our friendship over the years, the ultimate outcome of our original partnership cannot be denied: we had a phenomenal success with that first association.

There has been no really comprehensive account of how it all started, when heads rolled, directors were chosen, titles changed. In the press 'histories' of the birth of the mouse that was to live to such a great age, there have been few references made to the able and highly experienced director, John Fernald, the first to be offered the job of staging the play. He turned it down. I was unaware of this fact. Another notable omission remains Roger

Furse, the original stage designer of the splendidly atmospheric set. He is best remembered today as a distinguished art designer for such films as Olivier's *Henry V, Hamlet* and *Richard III*, among others. His name, along with my own, mysteriously disappeared from the bills when the show's success (to which I like to think we had both made major contributions), was being proclaimed outside the theatre and in the popular press of the day.

One of the many myths concerning the play, was that Dickie Attenborough (who played the part of Detective Constable Trotter) was thought by Agatha Christie to be too small in stature for the part. This was untrue. A small consortium backed Peter Saunders, and either way Dickie was always going to be in it.

Our opening night was to be 6 October 1952 in Nottingham. The dress rehearsals were scheduled for the Sunday and Monday evenings before the opening. I remember Agatha sitting well back in the stalls, sometimes alone, occasionally with me. Always modestly unobtrusive at such times, she was professional enough never to speak directly to the actors except through me. At the final rehearsal she appeared quiet, making few comments, but as excited underneath, I suspect, as any of us were. In those far-off days there could be found in the theatre, the tradition of first-night telegrams, now no longer observed since the disappearance of proper telegrams. Everyone in the company would wire everyone else their good wishes. I had a telegram from Sheila and Dickie, 'Bless you for all your unbelievable help and guidance. We are both so grateful. Fondest love Sheila and Dickie'. And the producer, Peter Saunders, placed on record his 'grateful thanks for your untiring work'. Perhaps most interesting of all, as it was not part of the chumminess that is part and parcel of the theatre on such occasions, Agatha sent me a memento of that first night. Bearing the inscription, 'Many thanks for all your help, dear Peter', it was a leather-bound copy of her play, *Towards Zero*. She was keen to get me interested in directing this play later on, and obviously felt after our successful association at rehearsals, I was the right director for the job. (In fact, when it was finally produced by another director in the West End, the play had a short run, having been panned by the critics.)

The first night curtain finally rang down on *The Mousetrap* at the Theatre Royal Nottingham, and I went on stage to call a rehearsal for the next morning. After receiving notes on their performances and getting the rehearsal call, the cast went back to the little supper party that had been arranged for them at the local hotel where most of us were staying. Agatha Christie and her daughter, Mrs Hicks, were naturally among the party, as were the producer, Peter Saunders, the stage manager, Tony Huntley-Gordon, and his team of assistants, and all the cast, most of them making their own silent prediction as to the play's chances of success when it finally arrived in the West End after its provincial tour. Another myth that has been circulated down the years is that Agatha had private doubts about having 'fallen between two stools', those of comedy and crime thriller. If this was the case she was careful to keep such thoughts to herself. Certainly she was relaxed at the supper. The cast was quite cheerful and, following its reception by the audience, optimistic regarding the play's outcome.

A good deal later on, when we found ourselves alone together after midnight, I was to chat over the play's chances with Agatha. When asked how long I thought we had, I replied that at this juncture it was anybody's guess. *All* the directorial tricks had worked (an essential factor in making the pace, the rhythm and the tension tick over, without which no slender play such as *The Mousetrap* can succeed). Judging from the cordial reception, the number of curtains at the end, it stood a chance of a very healthy run indeed. And upon more than one occasion the producer has agreed with me here, and has been quoted as saying that judging from the applause at the end on the first night it would be possible for a hit, now that the 'tricks had worked'. We could look forward to the rest of the tour at big touring theatres – Oxford, Birmingham and other number-one venues, duplicating its success at Nottingham and elsewhere, before opening at the Ambassadors Theatre, London, in late November. In Peter Saunders's opinion we were able to arrive in the West End, 'well run in, greased and highly polished'.

At the next day's rehearsal I tightened a few dull patches where the action might have appeared less lively than in other sequences, and eliminated any possible laughter that could lessen the tension. I suggested some possible rewrites, and even cuts to Agatha. She agreed with me that these would help the thriller side work better. There were still plenty of laughs to keep the humour intact, and she promised to make these few revisions put to her. (See Appendix 7)

The Mousetrap as an attraction nowadays rivals such institutions as The Changing of the Guard, The Trooping of the Colour, and the Armistice Day Service in November, the same month that saw the opening of 'the little thriller' that was to register the world's longest run. This fact is the more astounding when you hear what actors and actresses say about performing the lines. Mary Law, whose quotation opens this chapter, was very succinct; she did, after all, take over from Sheila Sim when Sheila left the leading role. However, writer and actress Diana Bishop is even more trenchant:

> Having gone so far as to take the plays of A. Christie out of the library to remind myself why, since those distant repertory days, I have remembered them with such hatred, after many false starts and swift glances (but not so many as in the texts) I knew. Everything about them is quite unspeakable, not least the dialogue. However, they are actor-proof since good or even brilliant actors appear uniformly mediocre.

One might of course agree with Diana Bishop about the dialogue. Right down the years many actors have thought likewise, without perhaps being able to express their dislike as cogently as she does. However, I think she missed a point in her castigation of Christie's dialogue: the author's ability to create scenes which offer scope to a director capable of creating a sense of tension, and able to ring the changes, enhancing each scene by his efforts.

Christie creates the situations masterfully; it only takes the judicial inclusion of a little currently colloquial language to put that which was stilted and sometimes false into some sort of order. One managed to do this during the rehearsal period with the whole-hearted consent and co-operation of the writer herself.

The Mousetrap has been called 'the best bad play ever produced'. But that does it an injustice. Any play that appeals to so many audiences for so long has, at least, to be a shrewd one, containing almost every element that might appear on a preview audience's check-list. As a piece of construction there wasn't any excess flab on it. The tempo – thanks to that ruthless cutting agreed between writer and director – was as near perfect as dammit.

For the most part, after its opening, director and writer corresponded rather than met. This was due to Agatha's departure for her home and novel-writing, soon after the Nottingham week. Meanwhile, I was just about to start directing another thriller in the provinces titled, *The Man*, again a play of tension, which would open almost simultaneously with *The Mousetrap* in London's West End. It was necessary for me to cross country from wherever *The Man* was playing to wherever *The Mousetrap* was playing. Glasgow, Manchester, Oxford; in many of these *The Man* played, in weeks before and following *The Mousetrap*. I covered long as well as short distances, to keep an eye on each production before they both appeared in London, where they were opening respectively at the Ambassadors, in the case of *The Mousetrap* and Her Majesty's, in the case of *The Man*. Rehearsals of both were held when they were needed, but fortunately both productions improved with playing in.

Incidentally, it is a strongly held belief of mine, one which I have always striven to act upon, that a director should never leave his production *completely* once it is launched. Sometimes it is necessary to take the odd trip away from England for a short while. This is a practice regularly adopted by some of my most active contemporaries. They have often been known to leave productions in pursuit of contracts previously entered into in the USA, on the Continent, and even as far away as Australia. I feel a director should never leave his production if there are certain things still to be worked upon. However, when a director is inundated with work, as I was at this time (having two productions running side by side, and both of them running smoothly on their try-outs, in properly ordered and professional stages, as these two were) one leaves all subsequent routine and understudy rehearsals to the efficient stage director. And in Tony Huntley-Gordon I had a good and experienced lieutenant, who would insist upon implementing his director's instruction as laid down and agreed. The director is the 'captain on the bridge'; his lieutenants ensure the ship's smooth running.

'My little thriller', as its author once called it, opened in London on 25 November 1952. It got a good press. In fact, for a slender play, when put to the test, it was a very good press indeed. (See Appendix 8)

It can be argued that the opinions expressed by influential critics are only personal ones. However, it seems to me that it is never right to suppress an opinion, especially if strongly held opinions are deemed to be sound ones. If they are false, of course, the harm can be that of confusion, convincing many through a long passage of time that any confusion contains an important truth. Here, the truth might have been said to be established by the unanimity of production bouquets hurled at the director of that original production.

Later, one of Dame Agatha Christie's biographers was to write: 'There is always a mystery surrounding anything to do with Agatha Christie, so it is not surprising that the two Peters, Saunders and Cotes, fell out.' It is true that we, who had worked together in harmony, fell out a fortnight or so after the play's première in London. Gwen Robyns, author of *The Mystery of Agatha Christie* (1978), went on to record the fracas between producer and director thus:

> What then could possibly have gone wrong between them?
> With his production running smoothly, and having recouped
> its production cost before it reached the West End, Peter Cotes
> absented himself, a customary procedure among busy theatre
> directors when necessary, for a few weeks in New York where
> he was booked already to direct the Broadway production of
> his London success, *A Pin to See the Peepshow*, starring Joan
> Miller. The fact had been publicised, over here as well as in
> America, and was known to both cast and management well in
> advance of Peter Cotes' production abroad.

So far so good, as the old saying goes. Imagine my surprise when, upon my arrival in New York, I received a cable from my agent, to the effect that I would no longer be welcome at the Ambassadors Theatre upon my return.

The miserable offshoot of this contretemps is that when the

play has celebrated its various 'landmark birthdays', the director who initially breathed work and energy into it, has not been invited to join the celebrations; a fact not unnoticed by Agatha Christie, who on the sixth anniversary of her 'little thriller' sent me a bound volume of the play signed, 'On our sixth anniversary, Love, Agatha'. Hubert Gregg (one of the many directors called in annually to redirect, yet again, my original production) makes an interesting point later in his book, *Agatha Christie and All That Mousetrap*. After saying the honouring of Christie had gone on and on he observes that 'As a matter of fact the one who should be up there (in the honouring) is Peter Cotes. He was the original director of *The Mousetrap* and I, for one, thought he did a bloody good job of it.' Well yes, maybe. Certainly it's all a long time ago now, and nothing can alter the fact that I am the *original* director any more than it can be disputed that Peter Saunders was the original producer, or that Agatha Christie was the original author. The fact is carved in letters of stone for the delectation of those still to be born, the publishers of the play, and historians of the past, as well as the future.

Down the years, there have been those who mistook, or chose to misunderstand the true situation. But whenever possible, I have stated the facts. (See Appendix 9) Silence in the face of calumny lends credence to what is spoken, shouted and written, for it will become henceforth a case of '*fact*, he hasn't denied it'. And from hints and murmurings and whispered confidences, yet another untruth joins the list of lies marauding as truths, now in the public domain. One's self-esteem evaporates as more uncorrected falsehoods support the charges made against the victim of what all too frequently becomes a concerted chorus of disapproval, unless checked. When mugged by the media, the victim feels bound to observe a reluctant silence – often through intimidation. But there are exceptions, as Shakespeare's Julius Caesar was at pains to point out in his dealing with honour and reputation long ago.

It has been said that some are born great, some become great, and others have greatness thrust upon them. So it is with litigation, when those who are not naturally litigious have litigation thrust upon them, even if only because they loathe injustice and refuse to see it conquer truth unrefuted.

Such has often been my position down the years when, rankling against a slur on my reputation, I have sought to redress a fib that has been put about and has finally become part of common currency.

Saunders's attitude towards me had only changed after the safe opening of the West End production and my enforced absence from London to fulfil a contract I had entered into some months earlier to direct *A Pin to See the Peepshow* on Broadway. By then, *The Mousetrap* had reaped a harvest of good press notices, the majority of which were more than civil to its director. The box-office takings were excellent and bookings extended well into the future. However, the manager's demands that I be barred from overhauling my own production from time to time if thought necessary – which I heard about when I was out of the country – and the unflattering remarks that he was making behind my back to certain sections of the press, have baffled many people down the years. I have personally thought such an attitude indicated 'sour grapes' because of my several adamant refusals to be bought out of my contract which consists of royalties of box-office takings. The idea was that I should surrender the royalties for an agreed sum of money. The offers were made finally through my agent, but earlier still by Saunders or his agent in negotiation. His justification for wanting this was my short absence in New York in 1953. Having heard my decision, the 'whispering campaign' started against me, and upon receipt of several untruthful and spiteful remarks (duly recounted by my agent), I wrote to the latter, on the 16 May 1958, as follows:

Eric Glass   from Peter Cotes
Piccadilly House   48 Limerston St
London SW1   Chelsea, London SW10

Dear Eric,

The Mousetrap
Altho' determined to continue this senseless vendetta,
Saunders must know how unjustified his attitude is. He
ought to be extraordinarily grateful for my contribution
towards the success of his play. I don't want to blow my
own trumpet but he knows enough about the theatre –
despite a shorter and possibly less impressive 'track record'

than my own – to realise how important it was and what benefits he derived from it. In any event, I am not prepared to allow anyone to write of me that I have 'quite lamentably failed in my obligations'. This is an untruth and is seriously damaging to me, even if written to you who knows how untrue and ridiculous it is.

My first requirement, therefore, is that you make it quite plain to him that this assertion must be withdrawn or I will consult my solicitors. My second point is that I am not prepared to have my production attributed to anyone else. My contract provides for my having a credit and there has been no break in the presentation of the play, so that it is my production which is being shown. If he likes to give a secondary credit to some other Director who may have worked on the play since – solely because he has not wanted me to do so – that is a matter for him.

May I end by saying it is too ridiculous that where a success of this sort has been achieved the Management should act in this way towards a person who has participated in creating the success. It is ungenerous and in my view foolish, and I hope you will contrive to impress this upon him.

I do not want to be drawn into legal battles with him or anyone else, but I will not hesitate for a moment if assertions of this kind, at the expense of a reputation that has been built up over the years, are irresponsibly made.

> Yours sincerely,
> Peter Cotes

But despite the letter and the silence that followed at first, this 'spoiling for a fight' attitude must have been simmering for quite some while. Even earlier on, when Richard Attenborough was on the point of leaving the production after his two-year contract with it had expired in 1954, he suddenly visited me in my production office in Jermyn St for what was ostensibly a social chat. However, it turned out to have a more businesslike connotation.

Dickie started off by giving me his customary friendly embrace. He reminded me that he was leaving the show shortly after his pre-arranged stint with 'Old Moneybags' – as he was fond of calling our manager behind his back – and that without his name in the cast there might well be a decided drop in the box-office takings. 'Therefore, old dear,' (or it could have been 'old darling' – I forget which) 'why not take a lump sum down from Old Moneybags, as a sort of down payment in lieu of your director's royalties, just in case the show's suddenly withdrawn?' The inference was, I suppose, that because Dickie had a financial interest in the show, he *must* know something? Dear Dickie! Well, whether he came as part of a one-man delegation or off his own (friendly) bat, I shall never know. Certainly, while he was persuasively nodding his good-natured head, I was just as definitely (if more slowly) shaking mine. I finally let him know flatly that I'd rely upon my contract and take my chance along with the other investors in the original production, most of whom had invested financially. My investment had been my *talent*. We parted on a cheery note, with Dickie being reminded of what he already knew only too well – that the play's run had been long in profit and there could be no financial losers after that. He took my point.

But despite this warning, which was followed by temporary moments of truce, Saunders was to lose few opportunities of resurrecting the myth that it was *his* talks with Agatha Christie (apparently without the presence or approval of the director, who was being bypassed in the matter) after the opening night in Nottingham, that wrought the miracle in the play's fortunes. Hey, presto! The miraculous effect of dropping a few lines here and there, and everything in the garden was lovely. . . . What could have been better than that it was effected with such ease? Not by the director – oh dear me, no – but by that very clever fellow, the manager.

Since these early occasional statements, which I have always refuted, I saw that the frustrated-director complex in Saunders's make-up must have got the upper hand, because he continued to treat fancy as fact when in 1972 he produced, in a book purporting to be his memoirs, an account of *The Mousetrap*'s beginnings that served to exclude me from any participation in the production's success and again made a number of unjustified allegations about my character.

However, weary of the eternal wrangle, and more worried by my wife's state of chronic ill-health than anything else, I let Master Saunders stew in his own juice. My anxiety then, as it was ever after until the time of her death, was that Joan's condition would be aggravated if I entered into a prolonged and costly legal battle. And this fact took precedence over all else, and prevented my instituting court proceedings against this tiresome fellow who apparently wanted a great measure of the artistic credit as well as the main financial reward. Nevertheless, I continued to rebut false statements whenever they arose, as the Appendices at the back of this book show. And as for silver linings; well, Billy Wilder, Hollywood director and wit, put it best when he once reminded me that 'Every time they build a better mousetrap, the mice get smarter, too. . . .' It's taken me a long time to realize that the 'softly-softly' approach doesn't work. Silence is the wrong way. It allows the other side to set the agenda.

ACT TWO:

Variations
Wilfrid Lawson
Oda Slobodskaya
Wee Georgie Wood
Joan Miller

Variations

The following portraits are all held together by a single strand – that which is loosely known as 'show-business'.

Ever since childhood I have taken an interest in those who are considered 'way out', the non-conformists of this world, some of whom I grew to know. Many of those I've known have already had biographies written about them. Others in this section of the book have not been so favoured. Belatedly, I strive to make amends for the short-sightedness of others, who have missed an opportunity by overlooking 'special' folk who have made their individual contributions to audiences all over the world.

If none of my subjects receive in-depth treatment, they are all bound together by the stuff of tragedy and in some cases, idiosyncrasy, gossip, and scandal. The theatre, music hall, and opera serve as backgrounds to 'characters', all larger-than-life, none of them typical, all of them out of the rut.

The four folk I write about in the following pages rose to be recognized in their lifetimes as out of the ordinary run of human beings. Permanent fame or notoriety is attached to certain names; but Wood (The Minute One), Lawson (The Boozer), and Slobodskaya (The Voice), have been largely forgotten since they died. That they who brought happiness and heartache to others, are now, alas, no longer with us, is a justification perhaps, for writing about them here. Their talents were great, but they deserve no mere hagiography. There were those who worked with and admired Wilfrid Lawson, who nevertheless resented him as inconsiderate, unreliable and disloyal.

All the unique people in the pages that follow, have been known to me closely, and these sketches are the unvarnished records of personal experience. Bound together, they represent a cast of characters which in any theatre programme must be adjudged unique, to say the least. They made the headlines once but were not accorded posthumous fame. These are fragments of biographies they were owed but never received.

Wilfrid Lawson – Drunken Thespian

The pathway through the long history of the theatre has been strewn with drunks: Edmund Kean, Barry Sullivan, Henry Ainley, the Barrymores, Laurette Taylor, Ion Swinley, Martin Walker, Peter O'Toole (who reputedly admits to being a reformed boozer), Robert Newton, Richard Harris. They have all led irregular lives. Some in their acting touched the heights, others became caricatures of themselves. Of my generation, perhaps the most notable of a notorious lot was the late great Wilfrid Lawson.

Wilfrid Lawson was a member of that little band of legendary figures who, for reasons hard to define, appeal to the imagination of the profession. Certainly, here was a performer whose unique capabilities combined to make him a bit like Jenny Hill's *The Vital Spark* or Shaw's *Life Force*, 'all in one piece'. He was an actor's actor, and is still, over twenty-five years after his death in 1966, a topic of innumerable anecdotes and the subject of folklore. London theatres didn't see him on their stages until 1929. He resurrected and recreated the magic that had been made part of theatre-going a generation earlier with the great Henry Irving. It is our loss that to date there has been no biography about this extraordinary man.

The time is the early thirties. Cedric Hardwicke, then our foremost male actor (later to became an actor-knight), was seated at a long trestled kitchen table set on the empty stage of the old Queen's Theatre in Shaftesbury Avenue. Hardwicke was to be *the* star in a cast of many others, about to start rehearsing a play with a circus background. The cast included famous players of that time, the Liveseys (Roger and Barrie), O.B. Clarence, Cecil Trouncer, and the redoubtable Maisie Gay, fresh from her early Noël Coward revue successes in the West End. The play, *Caravan*, was to have settings by Laura Knight RA (the painter of circus pictures), and the circus play, Carl Zuckmayer's continental success *Katerina Knie*, had been adapted from the German by Cicely Hamilton, a leading feminist of her day.

We were gathered around the table, flanked, I recall, by no less a figure than Bernard Shaw. Hardwicke was already known as a top Shavian actor, having scored successes in both *The Apple Cart* and *Too True to be Good* in the West End; hence G.B.S.'s presence as a close friend and professional associate of our producer, Sir Barry Jackson, founder and financier of the noted Birmingham Repertory Theatre.

We were well into this important first reading when suddenly there was a terrible clatter from the back of the stage near an outer door that led to the dressing rooms. The youthful 'unknown' with a minor role in the piece had arrived, an hour after everybody else. It was the first time I ever set eyes on the man who was to have such a pronounced influence upon my professional life in the years that followed. I say 'youthful' because he couldn't have been very much more than thirty at that time, although he had already been playing middle-aged and elderly characters in a number of classical productions in the provinces for some years past. Amazingly, despite his rackety life over the next thirty years, he never seemed to alter in appearance nor in the unpredictability of his character. Now he presented an astonishing sight, this spare man, with the sort of face that looks dried up with congealed blood. The eyes as he surveyed the occupants at the table were piggy and bloodshot. I took in the fact that he was wearing a beret as headgear and an army-type raincoat, very dirty, very old, with equally old frayed grey flannel trousers with bicycle clips showing underneath. He was wheeling an ancient bicycle, and mumbled as though talking to himself as he cast the bike against a backstage wall where it clattered to the ground.

I have never forgotten my first impression of this extraordinary creature. I forget whether he apologized publicly, there and then. Doubtless he did privately. The assembled cast and stage management, not to mention G.B.S. and Barry Jackson, shared mixed curiosity with downright disbelief at the sight of the man who had breached theatrical tradition (more rigid then than it is today) by being late upon such an important occasion. Still, Barry Jackson must already have seen him act (with Macdona) to engage him, and Shaw likewise, as Lawson had played a large number of Shavian roles for the Macdona Players who specialized in Shaw plays in the provinces, between the wars. And so an embarrassed stage-manager, holding the script with trembling hands, continued from where we had left off, with Lawson now sitting mute, as the Water Bailiff in the script (his part) had already been passed, and foregoing the chance of reading the whole script until the first rehearsal, which was scheduled for the next day. It was a bad beginning, but like so many other things about Lawson, as I was to discover, it was typical.

In the weeks that followed before the West End opening and until we went on our try-out tour, my meetings with him were only at rehearsals; later, however, as the junior member of the cast, I was compelled to dress with him. Nobody else would, and in those days only stars had dressing rooms to themselves. He mumbled to himself a lot, and always addressed me as 'Boy', bidding me 'do this and do that'. I found him terrifying; having as a boy actor been brought up in a theatre where discipline was the order of the day, I could not make head nor tail of this imperious and erratic man.

I grew to know him better, however, through seeing him at a considerable disadvantage one night. The production was embarking on its tour, prior to opening at Jackson's own West End theatre, the Queen's. We were to try out first at the King's Theatre Glasgow, and because of the busy schedules of that period, on railways and in theatres, it was necessary to travel by night for our first week's engagement. Theatre travelling arrangements in the shape of 'train calls' were vastly different then, and compartments of bunks had four persons accommodated to a carriage. The train rolled out of King's Cross for Scotland around midnight. I was on a bunk on the lower side opposite a slumbering Lawson, whilst above us were Roger Livesey (later to become a star in his own right), and another admirable actor, Cecil Trouncer. We were crossing that famous bridge between Newcastle and Edinburgh, with a certain amount of snoring from all four bunks, when suddenly there was a terrible cry of anguish from the lower bunk opposite me. I was later to witness other, similar incidents down the years, but at that time it was my first sight of an epileptic fit. Our fellow passengers were awakened to see what could be done for a recumbent Lawson who had not moved since his first frightening wail. We rallied round, but there was little we could do to get some reaction from our 'patient', who we now realized was an epileptic as well as an alcoholic. The little night-light, with a blue bulb, shone down upon this macabre scene as the train zigzagged on its way into Scotland. Looking back, it was providential that nobody thought to pull the emergency cord, because after what seemed an eternity Lawson recovered and we all resumed our former positions, although there was little sleep for anybody that night (with the exception of Willy, who after sitting up straight for a few moments, returned to his earlier sleeping posture without a word). Later I witnessed similar attacks in theatrical digs, dressing rooms and on film sets. At the end of each seizure he always returned to normal, apparently unaware and without knowledge of what had happened.

Lawson, who was born in Bradford in 1900, had been a bit of a juvenile delinquent at school, and had made his professional acting début during the First World War in *Trilby* at the West Pier Theatre, Brighton. He was sixteen. Later in the war he enlisted in the Royal Flying Corps and became a pilot. After being badly wounded by shrapnel, which came perilously near his brain, he was discharged as another wartime casualty. By 1919 he had resumed his acting career. During the next ten years, with various repertory and touring companies, including the distinguished Macdona Players, he performed more than 400 different parts. He was first seen in London at the Elephant and Castle Theatre in February 1928, in *Sweeney Todd*. Two years later, again with the Macdona Players, he was at the Royal Court in Sloane Square, performing in plays by Bernard Shaw which the playwright himself saw and approved. It was said of him at this time that he 'acted the rest of the experienced cast off the stage'! What an acting apprenticeship he'd had before that first afternoon I laid eyes on him. Alas, the production of *Caravan* did not run for long, although Lawson even then succeeded in collaring the notices in the comparatively small part of the Water Bailiff.

I saw Lawson play many other roles of varying size and importance on my frequent visits to the West End theatre. As a wide-eyed boy actor, I usually sat in the least expensive seats in the upper circle or the pit. I saw him once, in a charity matinée, do an Irving part, and I suddenly understood what Irving must have been like. I spent a good deal of my life in and around the theatre and I had read almost everything that had ever been written about Irving. I could never imagine, however, what it was like to watch him, until I saw Lawson do that extract. He fulfilled the entire part, whereas many other famous names have rattled about in their great parts like little peas in a big pod. They couldn't begin to fill the part because they were not great melodramatic actors. They had not the ability to swell out to whatever size the part required, which Lawson could and did. He was one of the few *great* actors I've ever seen in my life.

So, I had already acted with him and seen him in several plays from the audience viewpoint when he opened in 1937 at the Duchess Theatre in J.B. Priestley's *I Have Been Here Before*. James Agate (then the country's most influential critic), writing after the first night asked, 'Is this a great actor? Let me shelve the question by boldly stating that he is a grand one, whose present performance is something to dream about'.

It was also from the audience that I had seen him in *Gallows Glorious* at the old Shaftesbury. He was playing John Brown, the abolitionist, whose 'soul went marching on' in the famous song. Here, Lawson was on a small stage and appeared to be a big man (which he wasn't), larger–than–life-size. It was a most extraordinary performance, unlike any I'd ever seen before and I thought then, as I would think later, that his voice seemed to come from a distance. He seemed quite suddenly to appear from nowhere, take command of the stage and take command of the theatre in a triumphant performance.

The following year he was unwisely persuaded to play Antony to Mary Newcombe's Cleopatra at the Old Vic. Already raddled in feature, he was often inaudible; it was a performance perhaps better forgotten. He never again played Shakespeare. What a Lear was lost to us, what a Macbeth, what an Othello. . . . It was not much later that Grace Wyndham Goldie, writing in *The Listener* about a non-Shakespearean costume piece, marvelled that she had not seen the actor more often:

The King's Pirate was the only major piece I ever saw him in
and it was a very bad play, it didn't go very well. It was an
historical reconstruction of the latter part of the life of
Walter Raleigh . . . but not convincing anybody that it was a
historical reality, until Lawson came on, playing the
debauched, drunken horrible character of James I. Now I
don't believe any man was ever so horrible as Lawson
playing James I. He was absolutely unbelievable in every
detail of his reconstruction of that horrid personality who
filled the stage and made everybody else on the stage seem
like puppets. I find it impossible to write about it in any
way that does him justice or indeed, come to that, does me
justice. . . . Everything that he did, however tiny, seemed to
matter.

The King's Pirate was followed into the West End by *I Have Been
Here Before*. Priestley, in his book of short essays, *Particular Plea-
sures*, has described how Lawson had been sent along by his
agent to be considered for the part of the German in this play.
Priestley wrote, 'I had decided on a hunch that Lewis Casson
should play the German and asked Lawson to take on the
straight lead, Ormund, the North Country businessman. This
was his meat and he pounced upon it with a roar'.

Lawson entered films as early as 1935; his appearances included the role of a comic policeman in Carol Reed's *Bank
Holiday* and Doolittle in Anthony Asquith's *Pygmalion*. Early in
the war, when my brothers, the Boultings, were looking for an
actor to play the title role in their film, *Pastor Hall*, Lawson came
to mind. The one quality that he had evinced so clearly, in that
marvellous cameo in *Bank Holiday*, was quiet, controlled
strength; it was a comic role, but there was still that quietness
and suggested strength, and that was the deciding factor in his
casting as Pastor Hall. There were other factors. My brothers,
Roy who directed, and John who produced it, hadn't at the time
much money. . . . Here was an actor who had achieved a certain
name, a certain success, and he was within their purse. They had
a budget that would cover his salary, but there was another,
much more important reason. They didn't want to have in the
role of this rather heroic and noble gentleman, Pastor Hall, the
stereotype, the silver-haired pastor, or the man cast obviously

and physically in an heroic mould. They wanted somebody (the part was based on Pastor Niemüller) who could be identifiable as just an ordinary man, living in a grim Nazi world, for that was what the film was all about. The result gave Lawson a success in his first starring role in films. Through my role as a fellow-actor in that film I saw his part grow, and my brothers' hopes realized.

Soon after the Second World War started Lawson rejoined the Royal Air Force and on special leave went to Hollywood to appear in John Ford's film based on Eugene O'Neill's trilogy of one-act plays about the sea, *The Long Voyage Home*. A later request for leave to appear in another John Ford film, *How Green Was My Valley*, was refused, even though Lawson offered to hand over his Hollywood earnings to the Treasury. Lawson resigned his commission. There were other British films, other West End plays, but none of them did much for his reputation as a serious actor.

In 1947 he went to America to play the tyrannical Mr Barrett in a touring revival of *The Barretts of Wimpole Street*, with Katherine Cornell. He had played the part in London in 1935. There were frequent quarrels and the engagement came to an abrupt end. Lawson returned to England and seems to have disappeared.

In 1953 I decided to offer him the title role in a new production of Strindberg's *The Father* at the Arts Theatre Club. I made enquiries about exactly where he was playing rep and I took the train up to Oldham. He was not only playing two roles weekly but he was playing twice nightly: Monday, Tuesday and Wednesday as Doolittle, and Thursday, Friday and Saturday as Mr Barrett.

'Willy, I've come to offer you a job in the West End'. He only knew me as an actor, he'd never worked with me as a director.

'Oh, you direct nowadays,' he said rather disparagingly, 'you direct.'

'Yes, and I wish to goodness you'd come to my little theatre'.

We talked about this and that, and what he would like to do; he was full of ideas, and then I proposed *The Father*. Willy was unconvinced. 'What do you want to do Strindberg for? I should think it would empty every single seat in the theatre'.

'Not with you playing it.'

'Oh, shut up now,' he growled.

But I insisted. 'You'd be marvellous, the greatest actor in the country.'

We left it that he would let me know. But I knew when I went away that he was going to do it. And so began the most creative phase in his career. Willy would later call this 'my resurrection'.

A few weeks later the rehearsals began, with Beatrix Lehmann playing Laura, The Captain's wife. They were scheduled to start each morning at 8.30 instead of the more customary hour of 10.30, and I went through without any lunch break until 2.30. Willy after lunch was hopelessly drunk and so I received special dispensation from Equity for times of rehearsals to be changed.

When you gave him an idea he built on it. If you gave him a move he built on the move. He never got *out* of the play, he was *of* the play. There are many examples of his creativity. There is a scene in *The Father* between The Captain and Laura – their first big scene together – in which she casts doubt on their daughter's legitimacy, his little child. The two actors were going on and on; I had given them a few provisional moves and there were pauses. The tempo seemed good, when suddenly Willy stopped dead, leaning on the table. I thought, 'Oh my God. Willy's having another epileptic fit'. He didn't have an epileptic fit, he *acted* at having one. When it was all over he sat down, and looking at the floor said, 'Did you like that?' I asked, 'Are you going to do that, Willy?' He said, 'Do you want me to?' and Bea and I nodded in unison. He did it on the first night, and he did it every night. When people say that drink changed his performance nightly, I say he may have changed for certain directors, but he certainly never changed for me. He set his performance. . . . Mind you, he was more drunk on some nights than on others. I don't know whether he was drunk or sober when he *did* his 'fit' that particular morning, but he certainly gave a performance of having a fit. We had thought it was for real, but it was another example of his creativity as an actor. It owed little to the director, or to his fellow actor, except of course that Bea Lehmann was wonderful to play with. It was his actor's instinct that determined it was right at that moment, with his wife taunting about the illegitimacy, for him to react the way he did. It was dead right, he felt it in his heart and his mind; his actor's *being* told him so.

Trevor Howard was present at that first night and said later in a BBC radio interview, 'He had the ability to hit you right in the stomach and make you cry and I went out of my mind at the end of *The Father*. I just yelled the house down. I had never seen a better performance in my life. That still goes. But I can't tell you what he had, it was sheer magic'. At the final curtain, with Willy alone on the stage (Bea leaving the great actor to take his call as an isolated figure in the spotlight), Trevor was to rush from the back of the audience onto the stage, embrace and spontaneously kiss his idol – his favourite actor, on both cheeks – and that was how the final curtains were drawn on the two men, master and student.

After Willy's triumph, I asked him why in heaven he'd been away so long after returning from America, trailing around the provinces in any little repertory company he could get. He blamed it on the war. He claimed the war had brought in a lot of new youngsters who'd never heard of him, or if they had they didn't want to know. In his own words: 'They thought I was always pissed.'

After *The Father* came *The Wooden Dish* by an American, Edmund Morris. The critic, J.C. Trewin, noted in my BBC radio broadcast:

> Lawson played a veteran American, about 80, in a small
> Texas town, dreading a time when he might be sent to a
> home for the aged, and he had throughout to fight his
> inflexible daughter-in-law. And it was one of the most
> moving experiences we'd had in the theatre at that time to
> watch and listen to Lawson's inarticulate struggling,
> hopeless fight against fate. I think that the performances of
> the two protagonists, Lawson himself and Joan Miller, were
> quite overwhelming. So *The Wooden Dish* is always for me gold
> in the memory.

There has always been a great desire on the part of certain people, whether they be directors, actors, producers, dramatists big or small, talented or talentless, to dub their fellows with nicknames. Sometimes these names were obvious, sometimes they had a subtle connotation so that at first they did not resemble the recipient of the name at all. It was only later, when one delved deep, that one recognized the send-up. Willy would insist upon calling most of those to whom he was fondly attached, especially amongst those who played opposite him, by their made-up names. Clemence Dane, for instance, was 'the Great Dane', Beatrix Lehmann, 'the Old Owl'. Joan Miller, who played opposite him in *The Wooden Dish*, was christened 'The Maid', doubtless because he saw himself as Robin Hood in relation to Joan as Maid Marian. He liked to call me 'The Prod', Joe Losey was 'Joe Lousy', Helen Cherry, 'The Flowering One', and the playwright Rodney Ackland was known as 'The Ack'.

Willy Lawson earned his living as an actor in order to pay his bar bills. His film and television appearances were secondary, contracts entered into not so much to keep his name in front of the public as to make ends meet. Had he given the theatre a chance to be his occupation, his hobby, his love instead of his living, he might actually have enjoyed what he was doing. But as he didn't like anything so much as putting back the drink, the theatre became a prelude for him, down the years, to that time each day when he could pop into the pub next door. (Ironically Lawson was named by his teetotal parents after the Bradford temperance crusader, Sir Wilfrid Lawson. His real name was Wilfrid Worsnop but he later dropped the Worsnop in favour of Lawson as an acting pseudonym.) Some assert that he was the greatest British actor of his century. When my programme *This Fabulous Genius* was transmitted in 1981 on BBC Radio 3, it was pointed out by more than one distinguished participant to the programme, that he was exactly that. Many people, like Grace Wyndham Goldie, Bridget Boland, and Trevor Howard, were quite unable to say *what* made Lawson great, but great he certainly was.

Lawson's genius was such that whichever part he was playing, it didn't matter that not every word was heard, because whatever he said and did could be understood. He could have been playing in a foreign language at times, but like the Berliner Ensemble, the original Irish players talking at their broadest, and the Habima Players acting in Hebrew, in whatever he said or did he was always impressive, always compelling and always credible.

It is not without interest that in the radio programme I have referred to, at least two thirds of those taking part would lapse into impersonations of Willy. He had certain features and marked characteristics, such as the voice and the walk, the mottled face that resembled an area of congealed blood, and 'the mouth through which words came in a strangulated purr' (as J.C. Trewin so imaginatively put it). No two impersonations were identical, but enough alike to make the listener know that it was the same man all the impersonators were mimicking. Trevor Howard, Bridget Boland, Donald Pleasance, Keith Dewhurst, Beatrix Lehmann, Cecil Wilson, John Boulting, Joan Miller, Joseph Losey, Leonard Rossiter and myself all found ourselves recalling the strange voice of that terrible, troublesome man. It helped one remember how he caught his audiences by the throat, and set stages ablaze when he played full out like a sailing ship of the old ocean type.

Among other things, Wilfrid Lawson behaved like a schizophrenic. Having an eye for the main chance, he nevertheless had a death-wish that made it well nigh impossible for him to stay for long on equable terms with those who not only admired and loved the actor but were also in a position to help him. A born anarchist, he hated authority, and indeed would never hesitate to cause a rumpus when he was in the mood to throw discretion to the winds, allowing his antipathy to come into all the relationships he had with almost everybody who crossed his path.

Wilfrid Lawson thought he was being clever, playing his cards well, when in the West End in the fifties he left *The Wooden Dish* at the Phoenix in which he'd made a thundering success opposite Joan Miller. He omitted to advise his fellow players or the management of the fact that he planned to go into another play for a more powerful company. The company, H.M. Tennent, were casting around to get a subsidiary role in *Bell, Book and Candle* filled by a more or less run-of-the-mill character actor who would support two well-known actors, Lilli Palmer and Rex Harrison (better known at that time as film stars). Willy, with a child-like ingenuousness, affected surprise when the rest of the cast of *The Wooden Dish* felt left in the lurch when he departed. They had found out through reading the press, that because Lawson was leaving *The Wooden Dish* company it was being withdrawn. And this, despite the fact that business was getting better (it had opened in a heat-wave), the strength of the play's reception constantly growing following wonderful reviews, and word-of-mouth recommendations bringing in more people who were cheering at every final curtain-call. Further, the cast had made a united agreement to go on minimum Equity salaries to keep the piece running. Each member had thus made a sacrifice that was ungratefully rejected.

Such was his unquenchable thirst for drink that the man, Willy, was now short-changing the actor, Lawson. To have money in his pocket to pay for the booze was his principal consideration. It was more important by far than to continue to have his name outside the Phoenix Theatre co-starring with Joan Miller (his first star-billing in the commercial theatre during his long career). Just so long as he could buy his large tots of Scotch, followed by pints of Worthington as chasers, he seemed reasonably happy. He had no long-term point of view.

But drunk or sober, he could keep his audiences glued to their seats. Willy never seemed to mind much about the length of the runs he played in, so long as he was in work and he could go from job to job without feeling the permanent insecurity that seems to be the lot of most actors. *Caravan*, at the old Queen's Theatre, ran for only four performances, despite its all-star cast; *John Brown's Body* (re-titled *Gallows Glorious*) at the Shaftesbury Theatre barely reached the end of its second week; a revival of *The Barretts of Wimpole Street* at the Piccadilly (Willy playing the role created by Cedric Hardwicke a few years earlier) lasted for a very limited season. There were others as well.

To Willy all runs were a bonus. His greatest hit, in *The Father*, played only its bare three weeks at the little Arts Theatre Club although all theatrical London had flocked to see what became briefly a talking point. Lovat Fraser, of the Laurence Olivier Office, was sent to negotiate for a transfer to the St James's (urgently needed by that theatre following the financially unsuccessful season of the two Olivier-Leigh Cleopatra plays), to save it from expensive 'darkness'. With summer approaching, Willy (albeit an unfashionable actor) was now the talk of the town. The production of *The Father* was in progress, and with a small cast, all of them names, the proposition seemed good from all angles. The West End press had been phenomenal.

It was a tragedy, only a little less poignant than Strindberg's, that the deal fell through. Alec Clunes, who ran the Arts (better than it was ever run after his reign ceased), wanted it; as the play's director I was naturally delighted, and the cast were, to say the least, overjoyed by the news of an additional season to be played at the lovely St James's Theatre. Only Willy provided the question mark. His reasons were not always obvious, and perhaps he felt completely satisfied by his own great personal success. Having achieved what he'd worked for on a little theatre salary it was now a question of 'enough is enough'. When Willy supported Rex Harrison in *Bell, Book and Candle*, and Alec Guinness in *The Prisoner* (both in the West End and following *The Father*), it is quite possible that he simply enjoyed supporting others. It meant he did not have the responsibility of carrying a show, yet he could take away at the end of each week as a supporting actor a sizeable pay-packet (the star attraction being a box-office actor, something that Willy was never, alas, to become).

It is a matter of speculation as to how insecure this 'outsize' in actors was, how much he feared being the head of any company that he graced just in case there might be disgrace round the corner. He seemed unable to avoid the scenes, the arrests and nights in cells, and appearances in magistrates' courts. There were occasions when he was so 'blind' that he could use four-letter words in stage whispers (heard by his resigned fellow players, but rejected when heard by a disbelieving audience, so carried away were they that nothing outside the play's plot need be accepted).

As one who had disliked discipline from his youth onwards, he was inclined to favour the limited run, when he did not have to come up against a strict stage management. Most stage-managers who attempted to carpet Willy usually found themselves on the losing side, and unless the cast was solidly behind a firm director's production, the stage-manager had difficulty in seeing that the initial production was implemented. The end of the corridor always had to be seen, and unless Willy saw that light signifying another job to follow the current limited run, he would give his appetite for mischief full reign. Directors had to deserve, by their own behaviour, loyalty from a cast, and then Willy might be intimidated by a united front. The littlest weakness from any one quarter – management, stage-management, cast or director – and the proverbial cat (in Willy's case, it was a playfully troublesome bull mastiff, rather than anything so stealthy as a cat) would be among the pigeons.

Backstage he was irresponsible, on stage he was, from the audience's view, both in the part he was playing and the plot being acted out, the completely odd but responsible player. Erratic and eccentric in characterization (because that was his style of acting), he was, nevertheless, always the great professional. Even when tipsy his professionalism had the upper hand, and one could never be certain whether he was very drunk or merely sober with a hangover. If he spoilt, as he sometimes tended to do when in one of his most wicked moods, the performance of his fellow actors, he compensated for this by his own performance, which was always, drunk or sober, spot-on. He marked a part, enlarging upon it by polishing and building to momentous heights. Always he remained in his own role within the framework of the play, confining himself to the performance he had marked, with the approval of the firm director he tolerated and his wonderful actor's instinct. Of course he was always larger than life, whether life was a battleground or a slumbering interlude.

Grace Wyndham Goldie, the legendary BBC TV programme planner, in an interview about him cited Charlotte Brontë's masterpiece of drama criticism (an account of a performance by that other genius, Rachel, in Brontë's novel *Villette*), and suggests that it is necessary to have the genius of a Brontë to do justice to the acting of a Lawson. Not that there have been that many Lawsons, as Mrs Goldie recalls, and her own humility when reaching for an adequate description to suit the occasion leaves me with precisely the same feeling of inadequacy when writing about an actor who was a genius. Eric Shorter wrote in the *Daily Telegraph* on the same point recently:

Big acting is what we used to have. Or so they tell us. Some of us can even remember it. Scale was the thing. It stretched not only the player but also our imagination. That was another thing, our imagination.

Most modern acting doesn't try to. It strains for realism.

It often achieves it. The verisimilitude is amazing. . . . But there is another kind, and it is growing in scarcity. This is devoid of realism in the merely photographic sense. It isn't afraid to risk prosaic implausibility. . . . Such acting rises realms above impersonation. It invades our imagination. It takes it prisoner. It is acting with a capital A and there isn't any longer very much of it about. I wish I knew why.

Nor is it acting from the age of Henry Irving, which so few of us can hope, with precision, to remember, if at all. It is acting though, which has echoes of that age. It rises above reality. It catches hold of the imagination and enthrals it. It lights a flame you can't forget.

Is it because our taste in acting has changed or because the actors are no longer able, for various reasons connected with the size of theatre, to stir us as they did?

Willy was of course a disreputable chap, but as an actor he was paid the highest honour by his own profession, a memory that lingers on. He is still constantly discussed wherever his fellow actors continue to congregate; in pubs, on railway journeys, in dressing rooms, and in the few theatrical digs that still exist today, twenty-five years after his death. It's 'when Willy did this' or 'do you remember when Willy did that?' And then an oldish actor might come out with some outrageous memory; a tale that bears retelling because it's always new, especially if told by the type of story-teller who manages to remind one of so many of the quirks of this odd character who had so much to give as an actor, and gave so unstintingly during his limited life. Half a century was spent in the theatre, as well as the world of pubs, rehearsal rooms, agents' casting offices and touring. Many of the touring theatres had their stage doors adjoining pubs and here he could be found whenever he wasn't rehearsing, at the corner of the bar, back against the wall with his drink on the counter. Usually he would be gazing reflectively at it until he grasped the glass, lifting it to his lips, closing his eyes as he savoured the contents before ordering another, and another. . . .

He was not invited to play in radio very often because Lawson had to be seen, as well as heard, even if it was only to lip-read and note the expressions on that mottled, comic, beetroot face.

That face that encompassed the terrible and the tragic as it creased into so many different types of expressions.

He played tricks, and the wounds in his life were often inflicted upon his friends as well as his beloved wife, 'Girlie' (made deaf by a tragic drinking bout in which she had been the victim early in their marriage). But she went on loving him just the same, still hearing the voice of a young actor she had married many years earlier, before it became the croak and rasp of the man's excesses. G.B.S. once expressed the view that 'we're not dead if we're alive in the hearts of our friends'. To that extent then, Willy twenty-five years after his death, must still be very much alive today.

Wilfrid Lawson died, as old as the century, on 10 October 1966 three months short of his sixty-seventh birthday. His near contemporaries, John Gielgud, Laurence Olivier, Ralph Richardson, all of them were actors of a very different kind. Like another near contemporary, Donald Wolfit, Lawson belonged to what has been called 'the unfashionable theatre', and was described in part by Wolfit's biographer Ronald Harwood as 'that section of the theatrical profession, actors in particular, who are regarded by their fellow men with a mixture of grudging admiration, disdain, and often amusement. . . . The pity is that their contribution to their art is not fully acknowledged, for repeatedly it is these men who make secret inroads into the drama for others to proclaim publicly'. Wilfrid Lawson was of this company.

He occasionally did the odd TV play; one for me, with Peter Cushing and Bryan Forbes also in the cast, was *The Road*, an English adaptation of Jean Jacques Bernard's *Nationale 6*. As always he made his presence felt. In another telly drama by Keith Dewhurst, he played a very small part of a Puritan preacher who went onto the barricade to exhort the Parliamentary soldiers to fight harder. Dewhurst recalls,

He had one big speech in this piece which was about Christ being a working man. By this time he was very frail, he'd shrunk, the gleam in his eye had got much brighter. Fellow-actors during rehearsals gathered round whenever he was doing his speech to watch him acting; because they thought him totally miraculous, they came to pay tribute to his acting. It was a mark of respect. He was very disreputable, and he was really a failure in life, and he was a person who destroyed himself, but despite that, other actors would still go to see a man who could show that theirs was a noble art.

Joan Miller recalled that she saw the other side of his character as well: 'I never heard him say one single word against another actor. I have hardly known an actor not say *something* about other actors. He hardly knew they existed, he couldn't be jealous because he was so much bigger, he was so much better.'

Beatrix Lehmann was later to confess,

I always thought he was potentially the greatest actor of his age. In a curious way he wasn't entirely of his age because you've got to remember that in previous generations there'd been people like Herbert Tree, Johnston Forbes-Robertson who in many ways had changed the old way of speaking and declaiming which belonged to Irving. Well, Wilfrid had this declaiming voice and the onomatopoeic that was used in the time of Irving, and yet behind it was this tremendous burning personality that came pouring over, and I can still hear his voice in my ears because I'm glad to say we had a very good relationship, partly because he was almost incapable of dressing himself, so I dressed him and I used to go and see that he was decent before he went on stage. He didn't mind this a bit, he was delighted and got very upset if I was late in coming in to do up his buttons, and he always referred to me as his old owl, which was, I gathered, the owl of wisdom.

And then he'd say to me, 'I'm going to give so-and-so a "run round" tonight.' And a 'run round' meant that in the middle of the script when it came to a cue or a question usually addressed to a young and trembling actor, he would put in an obscenity, and put them on the spot because they didn't know what to say. So they used to come pouring into my dressing room, saying 'Oh for God's sake tell me who's going to have the "run round" tonight?'

He only tried it once on me, and I saw the glint in his eye, but I can't remember the exact lines. . . . 'Laura, Laura, oh when we were young and you took me in the woods and

the fields, and told me the names of the flowers and what
the bulls did to the cows. . . .' and this extremely wicked
look came over his face and I thought 'I've got you now,'
because he had to go on with the speech, it wasn't a
question mark. Afterwards I went into his dressing room
and I said, 'Look Wilf, one more of those to me and I don't
dress you, and you'll be arrested for indecent exposure.'

Of course it's impossible to say what is greatness in an
actor. I think it's a kind of sympathetic imagination,
somebody who is able to really put themselves in somebody
else's shoes. It seemed to me it was playing a person so truly
that they became huge. They became bigger than anybody
else. I don't mean that he was elbowing everybody else off
the stage, but it became a great important memorable
performance. If he'd played two lines he probably could
have done the same thing because of the reality of it. I don't
mean naturalism alone, it wasn't just that. In fact he was
never naturalistic, not realistic ever. It was just *true*, that's
all. He was true and that made him great.

In his audiences Lawson managed to create a tension, a
feeling that they must watch him, come what may. I have a clear
memory of him working this magic in very difficult circumstances. The play was almost four hours long, the weather
baking, and no air-conditioning as today. Lawson came
on towards the end and this steamy, restless, exhausted audience
held its breath: you could have heard a pin drop.

It's hard to say how the historian of the future will remember
Lawson. I've always thought of him as a man alone, a man
apart, almost a man from nowhere who suddenly possessed an
audience, possessed a part, possessed a play. I think that that is
a splendour of achievement, and to me he meant much more
than any of his most acclaimed contemporaries. I remember that
voice best from one of his last performances. He was in *Peer Gynt*
at the Old Vic in the sixties. He always had the power to hold
the audience in silence, as towards the end of that long straggling
night when Willy, as The Button-Moulder, appeared with the
concentrated glare that he so often used.

I know I went from the theatre remembering not Peer's major speeches but Lawson's simple line, 'Remember we meet at the next crossroads'.

Unhappily, I never met him again at any crossroads, but as with John Brown, his 'soul goes marching on'.

ODA SLOBODSKAYA

The Duchess of Baker Street

'The Duchess', as she was called towards the end of her days, was London's very own prima donna. There was some fuss made some years ago about a television series called 'The Duchess of Duke Street', which purported to be based upon the life and loves of the notorious hotelier and flamboyant friend of monarchs, Rosa Lewis. But Oda Slobodskaya, one of the great sopranos of the twentieth century, knocked Rosa into a cocked hat for bigness of character, personality and talent.

Slobodskaya was born in 1888, the same year as Maggie Teyte, Lotte Lehmann and Frida Leider; her parents were Jewish shop-keepers in a small town in Tsarist Russia, and from there she won a scholarship to the St Petersburg Conservatoire. She graduated and soon became leading soprano at the Marynsky Theatre, but a potentially brilliant career was stopped by the Revolution and she fled to Paris, caught the eye of Diaghilev and was cast by him to play Parasha in Stravinsky's *Mavra*.

Arriving eventually in England, she turned her undoubted powers, a remarkable voice and personality, to good use on the then still thriving music halls. She used the pseudonym of Odali Careno and commuted between London and New York as a variety headliner, making appearances under her own name whenever the golden opportunity arose to play a role in opera that gave scope for her talents. Increasingly well known and with money put by, she re-adopted the Oda and dropped Odali. In great demand as an opera singer, she gave recitals throughout England and America during the twenties and thirties. Later, her career was to take a nosedive and to future generations she would become an unknown, largely because of the neglect of the recording companies for whom she had made many highly praised discs (HMV, in particular, in 1931).

But if Slobodskaya's talents waned towards the end of a long life that was richly rewarding for those music lovers who heard her in her heyday, when she sang under the baton of such conductors as Beecham and Fistoulari, her greatness of character never lessened.

She could be seen frequently towards the end, shopping in Baker Street, striding along a pathway in Regent's Park. An unforgettable figure, she marched, rather than walked, with head held high and eyes that peered, through age, where previously they had shone. No longer the prima donna (for she had fewer stages towards the end upon which to exercise those particular tantrums associated with prima donnas), she still possessed a hauteur of the type of grand duchess so frequently depicted in stage plays and comic operas.

Oda Slobodskaya was indeed a 'somebody' from the start – and she remained so to the end. I first saw her from afar in the mid-forties whilst queuing for a no. 13 bus. The services then were no better than now, and I was one of a crowd of stragglers who had waited in a long line for over half an hour. Suddenly a large, imposing woman with a white face, heavily made-up clownlike lips, baleful look, flowered garden-party hat and fur stole arrived late in the queue. Jumping her place as though by some divine right, and ignoring the muttered protest of the rest of us and the audible growls of those at the very head of the queue, she stepped smartly onto the bus that finally arrived. While everybody clustered round to follow on, the conductor called, 'Only one, please'. That *one* was Oda, the Big Woman who swept ceremoniously inside the bus as it restarted, leaving a mutinous crowd to await the next no. 13, whenever it chose to arrive.

The first encounter was to be remembered by me, when some months later I was presented (for nobody was ever less than 'presented' to her) to an impressively dignified Madame Slobodskaya. Her reputation as a soprano had been known to so many of us down the years, but those formidable features had not been recognized that day when she so nearly caused a minor revolution in Finchley Road by her skilful 'jumpin' of the bus queue. As the months progressed, I was to meet her socially upon many further occasions, several times at the flat of my mother, who lived in the same purpose-built block of flats off Baker Street, where Oda had an apartment.

In the daytime she nearly always looked as though she were dressed for the Royal enclosure at Ascot; most nights as though she was just about to step onto the platform at an opera house. An odd, majestic look; she reminded one of Margaret Dumont in build and personality, when that portly American actress was 'feeding' Groucho Marx.

The eminent music critic, Desmond Shawe-Taylor said of her that she was 'the outstanding interpreter of Russian song in this country – perhaps the world'. During the last twenty years of her life she was thought of as *passée* and something of a fallen star. This was shameful neglect on the part of the music establishment, as her voice, because of her early training, was in its way still unique.

I have memories, not just of her lovely singing but her colourful and generous personality. Once in the 1940s she graced a performance of Strindberg's *Miss Julie* (with Joan Miller in the tragic title role) at the Lyric, Hammersmith. It was a matinée performance in a London heatwave and the theatre was barely a third full. The production had been acclaimed by the critics but Strindberg by day, in humidity, daunted all but the most ardent theatre-goers. At the end however, when the cast took their calls, down the centre gangway marched Oda, proudly carrying a large bouquet for 'Miss Julie'. It could have been a Covent Garden opening rather than a London theatre in the suburbs. Life is certainly duller without her. I have never known such a forceful personality, or such a zest for life. How can one sum up her artistry? She had the ability of making words pregnant with meaning and getting to the heart of a work.

TV announced her death in 1970 on all the channels; Radios 3 and 4 devoted considerable time to her career as an important singer. Next day the quality newspapers both in England and abroad wrote at length in their obituary columns about the passing of one who was a great personality with an even greater voice. Sir Compton Mackenzie said over the air: 'such a glorious voice as this would make a poem of an Income Tax form'.

Her finale was tragedy greater than Mimi's in *La Bohème*. She suffered from ulcerated feet towards the end and before that was a chronic diabetic; these illnesses had grown progressively more tortuous. When gangrene set in, the ambulance was called to deposit her in hospital. There proved to be no alternative to having her foot amputated, although even that operation failed to arrest the fast-travelling infection. More amputations followed, until the whole leg was removed.

There seemed to be a period of remission then, before it was discovered that the other leg had become infected and had to go too. Refusing at first, and attempting to preserve the last remnants of her strength, the weakened Oda said No. But bit by bit surgeons, specialists and the nursing sisters around her, all took it in turn, some together, to persist. Their message was that if Oda would not let them operate, her system would be poisoned. There was no alternative, then, to the death that was already impending. Embattled with pain and no future outside hospital, did she ever contemplate voluntary euthanasia?

Even in her tragic state she fought mentally, employing words of doom to underline her despair; she summoned the strength to moan that she didn't want to live out her remaining life in a wheelchair. Nevertheless, almost the last words to reach the ears of her listeners were, 'Life is sweet'. A born fighter, she never became resigned, but finally gave her consent to her last battle being over.

The second leg was amputated. A short time later, the woman who talked about 'breadth, width and vocal delivery' in others – whether she was criticizing adversely or praising with passion – drew her last breath.

She died on 29 July 1970, and although it is well over twenty years ago now, she is vividly remembered, not only as a monumental character but as a divine singer of songs. Her epitaph was spoken by the few musicians and stragglers who gathered to see her off at Golders Green Crematorium, and since that time, by the distinguished accompanist, Ivor Newton, whose own partnership and friendship with Oda went back scores of years – since 1930, that period when Oda sang with Sir Thomas Beecham and her partner was Chaliapin at the Lyceum. Ivor Newton later recalled:

During the last terrible years of her life when lying in
hospital she was subject to bouts of agonising pain. I could
not but tell her how I admired her courage. 'When pain
comes' she used to say, 'I go through my repertoire – one
day Mussorgsky, another Rachmaninoff, another
Tchaikovsky, another Prokofiev. I grow so angry with myself
if I have forgotten a word. . . . I could not stand the pain
if it were not for that'. I have memories of her lovely
singing and colourful personality. Life is duller without her.
I have never known such a forceful personality, or such
a zest for life.

She had gone on into her late seventies, still determinedly
giving 'concerts' as she called her 'scratch' appearances in fit-ups
in small towns and village halls, far and wide; even when they
hurried her into hospital in her eighties for the last terrible time,
she started making plans from her sick bed – recital plans for her
recovery.

Her struggles are long over but her memorable recordings
have ensured that, as in the last speech of John Drinkwater's epic
play *Abraham Lincoln*, now she belongs to the ages.

WEE GEORGIE WOOD

The Weeny One

In England for many years music hall had an individual quality. It was in its prime before World War I, but throughout the war it continued to flourish and, in the twenties and thirties it changed its name to variety. This was due to an influx of American acts: Burns and Allen, Fields and Weber, Nora Bayes, Elsie Janis, Morton Downey, Georgie Jessel, Danny Kaye, Sophie Tucker. All came from American vaudeville, a derivative of variety. It's hard to end the headliners who came across and became stars of two continents. A few, like Bob Hope, Jack Benny and Judy Garland returned again and again. The Americans when merged with such English greats as Gracie Fields, Vesta Tilley, Marie Lloyd, George Robey, Robb Wilton and Wee Georgie Wood, provided remarkably good entertainment. It was hearty, robust, full of verve and sometimes even a kind of poetry. We miss it today, for the quality of this flesh-and-blood 'live' entertainment is not communicable by either television or radio.

Wee Georgie Wood. What a name to conjure with! One largely forgotten today, but in the twenties, thirties and forties, it was a vastly different matter. He turned his act into a theatre of magic, his work in various sketches being a shade of acting at its finest. One was warmed by his high-pitched treble voice, his childlike sense of pathos, neither of which could be successfully transferred to the screen. He made one or two films in his lengthy career, the best known being *The Black Hand Gang*, which he made at Elstree. The human contact was missing and his immense personal charm never made it to the big screen. This charm was a quality possessed by Wee Georgie Wood more than any other 'actor' in variety, with the possible exception of Albert Chevalier of *My Old Dutch* fame, and Bransby Williams with his repertoire of scenes from Charles Dickens.

The best music hall acts were strengthened and buoyed up by

the response from out-front. The artist heard the laughter and the silences, and a great rapport was built between the two, audience and entertainer. The laughter and applause created an oasis of loving mirth between stage and auditorium. It is impossible to feel such intimacy between a player and his television audience; shadows on screen and voices from box are the work of an editor, who at the flick of a switch can fade the sound up or down, thereby frequently spoiling the illusion. Timing is an actor's best friend, those that have it are touched by inspiration, or a sense of mere natural *feeling* and it is a quality often lost on the small screen.

The actors in variety had to make their impression on the audience immediately the curtain rose, but it was only in the last few moments of 'acts' that lasted between ten minutes and half an hour that the climax arrived. And so it was with Georgie, assisted by the portly Dolly Harmer as his mum (she was still his mum when he was over sixty!) that the surprise came in the last minute of a thirty-minute sketch. It was his stance, his influence through the still quality he exuded, that made the final onslaught on the emotions such a pinnacle. As it was, we were crying when Georgie took his playing from darkness to light and we laughed and clapped still more as he took his curtain. This was a specialized art and the audience was so engaged in having its emotions wrung that it failed to see the wheels going round. It was only the boy-actor who knew how it was done.

George Wood saw variety booming in the years between the wars and Wee Georgie Wood, when an elderly gentleman, had lived on to become one of its greatest glories.

The characters of yester-year were characters in their own right. They didn't dress distinctively nor talk raucously only to catch the eyes of the gossip columnists and TV interviewers. It was another world that bred them. When Georgie Wood died in the late seventies he left behind a legacy; one that was very precious and in an age when the unmistakable quality of personality seems almost to have vanished from the scene. He left a special gap. Georgie Wood liked to be referred to – it was a foible of his – as *Mr* George Wood. Although a Tynesider by birth he lived long enough in the metropolis to become part of the London 'scene'. If not one of the immortal Marie Lloyd's 'One of the

Ruins That Cromwell Knocked About a Bit', Wee Georgie, as he was to become known, never retired, not even when he'd stopped being a professional music hall headliner. He had a gift that had been in front of the public, up and down the country and in other countries as well, for nearly eighty years.

He started as a child performer in 1900 at the age of five and officially ended a great variety career well over half-a-century later. He bridged the gap between semi-retirement and his final curtain with appearances here there and everywhere, writing zesty gossip columns for first the old *Encore* and *The Performer* and later *The Stage*, for more than a score of years.

Telly personalities are encouraged to adopt telly attitudes and many of the latter are manufactured public relations stuff. But Wee Georgie was different. The man in the street would recognize and turn around to wink and head waiters would herald his entrance in a restaurant with special attention. Bus drivers called out 'Hello Georgie' or 'How you keeping, Guv?'. He was a character; one of those, like Lord Lonsdale and Prince Monolulu were on the race-course, Neville Cardus in the Long Room at Lord's, Hannen Swaffer in Fleet Street, and Charles B. Cochran at West End first nights. All of these exuded character, better known today, perhaps, as charisma, as much part of the permanent 'scene' of their day as the Beefeaters at the Tower of London and The Changing of the Guard, at Buckingham Palace.

Women played a predominant role, certain women, that is, in his life. The failure and subsequent annulment in 1932 of his four-year marriage, was a tragic blow to him. He cherished the memory of the variety star, Mona Vivian, all his life. Apart from his stage mum, Dolly Harmer, who was obviously important to him, there were also his two loyal housekeepers. Firstly there had been Bella Marshall, who shared his life for forty years, and latterly, his last housekeeper, Ethel Adams, who became his boon companion for the last fifteen years of his life. Ethel had been a keen fan before becoming his closest friend. Both she and Bella served loyally and faithfully the little fellow who was 'The Minute One' off stage and the perennial naughty boy on.

Georgie was a many-sided variety star, film actor, radio and television artiste. However, he shone his brightest as a multi-coloured live performer. He was probably a more colourful character off stage than he was on; his talent for pathos, however, was outstanding. I wrote at the time of his death, 'The variety stage loses its best legitimate actor since the death of Bransby Williams'.

A doughty crusader for many causes in his day, untiring as he was in every branch of living, Georgie always seemed to have energy to spare for voluntary service; no effort was withheld from what was considered a worthy cause. As long ago as 1936 he was installed King Rat of the Grand Order of Water Rats and many times after that he was one of that charitable order's preceptors. All things considered, his, when it came, was an exceptionally well earned OBE.

His learning was extensive and exceptional considering that he was completely self-educated. It has been said that he once completed a *Times* crossword in under ten minutes! In his general journalism he touched, and let go of, such problems as show-biz, moral rearmament, tycoonery, unsung talent, excessive power, publicity, conscience, false pride and corruption (in high and low places). These were subjects that he was on his hobby-horse about; sometimes strident and quick to take offence, he dealt with people and ideas both stupidly and sensibly. As well as his *Stage Jottings*, he wrote (a good deal less successfully) more than one autobiography. There were also his well-publicized discussions with 'names' from Al Capone to Bernard Shaw; the Pope to Frank Buchman and H.G. Wells. There was a hard core of steel revealed when he was arguing the toss.

In private life the public character was a careful companion, concealing his trusty heart as something that was too heavy a liability to carry around in such a small frame. Others took the little man at face-value, finding his occasional peevishness and arrogant censoriousness alarming. He was (when he emerged after some imaginary grievance from behind his emotional safety curtain) both human and endearing. Those who knew him as well as I did were unlikely to be deterred from recognizing the person behind the façade.

Many and varied are the stories told about his ancestry. When I one day queried the truth of some of these tall tales, he personally confirmed that he was born on 17 December 1895 weighing $8\frac{1}{4}$ lbs. at Jarrow-on-Tyne. The delivery took place in a bedroom over a pawnbroker's shop owned by his father. He was given the name of George Wood Banlett. His mother was Georgina, fourth daughter of George and Dorothy Wood. Apparently George and Dorothy had twenty-one children all told: three were stillborn, six died at an early age, but the other twelve, six sons and six daughters, lived to ages between seventy-three and ninety-one. 'I never knew my maternal grandmother,' he told me with a twinkle in his eyes, 'but I do remember seeing in the obituary compiled by my maternal grandfather the words, "God has called her from her labours"!' George Wood, this maternal grandfather, was a Sunderland master butcher whom George described as 'a good looking man, generous to a fault'. His struggle for good causes in what was a poor neighbourhood was well known. George was later to follow in his grandfather's footsteps. . . .

According to George, when he was only eleven weeks old his parents moved to South Shields where his father became the manager of a grocery shop, of the then prosperous Walter Willson chain.

Apparently both George's parents were of normal size, as indeed were all his ancestors with the exception of Charles Arthur Banlett, of Thirsk, in Scotland and Lille, in France. Banlett must have been nearly seven feet tall, judging by a picture of him standing by a combine-harvester, which he told all and sundry he had invented. Obviously there was a strain in this family of contrasts that never permitted its members to do things by half.

Just before George's fourth birthday it was discovered that this odd little offspring had an amazing talent. When he was read a recitation, he could repeat up to three hundred words of it by heart. Routledge's *Popular Reciter* was quickly purchased and that pocket reference book of the late nineteenth century helped him to acquire quite a repertoire of his own.

All the Wood family were said to be Nonconformists in matters spiritual and George's first religion was Methodism (he dabbled with many others after that). Early, he grasped his new 'toy' and soon was to be found sharing it and reciting in all the Methodist churches in the district. He recited *Billy's Rose, Don't Take My Dear Mother's Bible* and *The Dying Immigrant*, all with astonishing success and without missing a word. He was subsequently selected to recite and sing at the annual Methodist jamboree at Seaham Harbour; his mother's youngest sister, Aunt Maggie, being sent to take charge of him upon this occasion. He finished his contribution by singing a ballad called *Skylark* with the subtitle, 'If among the angels, Mother you should see, ask her if she will come down again to poor dear Dad and Me'. Thereupon Maggie threw a halfpenny on to the bandstand platform; this encouraged the audience to chip in with a shower of coins. It was his first professional appearance as an infant prodigy; one who never stopped being an 'infant prodigy' over the next seventy years. Aunt Maggie collected £12.2.6. from the platform. She spent the odd half-crown on buying him a small Goss china vase bearing the Seaham Harbour coat of arms to take to his mother. On their return home, his mother upset Aunt Maggie by hardly noticing the Goss china vase, but seizing avidly on the £12.0.0. That £12.0.0. probably deprived George of a normal childhood. It gave his mother ideas. . . .

Between the ages of six and nine he was sent out to earn money as a member of Will Elliot's then famous North Country concert party, The Sunderland Merry Mascots; The Bliss and Bliss Pierrots, in West Hartlepool, and with the Cosgrove and Burns Troupe at Barnard Castle. By the time George was ten (in the year 1906), he was the star of Levi and Cardwell's juvenile touring company. More importantly, his earnings were sufficient to enable his mother to divorce his father and marry Will Allon, a Sunderland police constable. 'We had the law as well as religion in our family,' George liked to remember.

From then onwards until his mother's death in 1946, he became a man with something to hide. 'Wee Georgie Wood' was a separate entity from George Wood, who in turn wanted *so* much to be George Banlett. Apparently, when he was performing in South Africa in 1909, without either his mother or stepfather in tow, he experienced a joy in his work that he was never to experience again when perfecting his performance techniques. In his early sketches on the halls his roles were 'baby' characters and this lasted until 1917, when he started a forty-year association as a professional team with Dolly Harmer. She played his 'mother' in innumerable sketches that became world famous.

Dolly died at the age of ninety-four, two weeks after completing a pantomime season with her stage 'son', who lived on without his 'feed' and was never to be seen to quite such good effect again. During their long association Dolly, always robust in speech and figure, tried to make him realize that being *Wee* Georgie Wood was a valuable trade mark. Finally after her death, he came to realize that she was right and, as Wee Georgie Wood, at 4 feet and 5 inches, show business continued to take him all over the world.

Nobody knew, until George revealed it much later, that ever since he was rejected in 1917 by the War Office Medical Board for military service, he had hated being small. Neither was he resigned to being different, if only in physique. Nor to the fact that such notabilities as Keats, Pope, Swinburne and Marat had all been diminutives. Contemporary stars of the music hall in the twenties were Tiny Mite, Daphne Pollard and Ivor Winter; Charlie Drake and Hilda Baker, both diminutives, came later; they were stars in the forties and fifties. These personalities quickly learned to make people laugh – and to laugh at themselves. Not so George. None of these mentioned was half as successful as George in his heyday. Yet he never became fully resigned to the curse of his height. When Noël Coward wrote in *Red Peppers*, his one-act playlet, 'I hate little men, their brains are too near their bottoms', there was one little man who took grave offence, who pretended to be unconcerned, but it rankled.

His worst moment came when at the age of nineteen he was advised by doctors that he had already stopped growing. A short time later he consulted a Dr Ebenezer Lawson, once a pupil of Jung, who told him of a certain Viennese professor who had been experimenting with 'miraculous' adjustment operations. Lawson later became apprehensive when George declared his intention of himself travelling to Vienna without delay. 'It's only in its infancy and could be dangerous and terribly expensive,' he warned. 'That doesn't matter', came the reply, 'I *am* going. I've no intention of living my life out like this.' He was at this time earning never less than £150 per week, which was a huge sum in those days. His mother, however, was the chancellor of *his* exchequer and his 'allowance' was pocket money at no more than 10s a week. This meant that the mysterious Austrian professor would be dead by the time he could afford his fee.

His personal problems were common to many of restricted growth. The heaviest burden of all was the denial of a formal education. And yet, when a very young man, George had been encouraged by the late Lord Birkett, better known as Norman Birkett K.C., to study law. But it was never practicable to stop being Wee Georgie Wood. And when The Minute One tried to write (to be read, if not seen), in an effort to be *somebody else*, all he could finally achieve as regular work was an offer to be a columnist on show-biz periodicals. Finally, as he grew older, he had to cut down on even this sideline in *The Stage*, although it was this organ of the profession (as this newspaper was widely known) that gave him a chance to confer with little Jimmy Clitheroe, also from the variety mould and another small man. Jimmy revealed, surprisingly, that he knew nothing about anything much, except stocks and shares; having made a fortune on the Stock Exchange. After Clitheroe's sudden death it was broadly hinted that it was suicide. 'It was nothing of the kind,' wrote George, 'the coroner's verdict was "death by misadventure"; his mother to whom he was devoted had died, the BBC had notified him they were terminating his series and he had not been sleeping well; barbiturates had been prescribed for him. On that last night Jimmy must have had a sense of contentment, for he had changed his will to make Cancer Research the main beneficiary.' In George's opinion, 'his overwhelming loneliness at being "different" had overcome Clitheroe. This time he had taken his sleeping pills with an extra strong "night-cap"'.

In fact, statistics show that midgets have a negligible suicide rate, yet odd incidents can drive them into deep depression. As for instance, when George heard such good friends as Charlie Chester and Ted Ray telling jokes like, 'Couldn't get to sleep last night. Wee Georgie Wood was in the top bunk and his pacing up and down gave me a headache'. And he never forgave Noël Coward for the hurt. Still, he was able to muster a half smile when the late Robb Wilton went public, congratulating Wee Georgie Wood because he'd just been made a Buffalo. A voice in the audience replied, topping Robb in a loud stage whisper, 'Buffalo, Buffalo, Christ he's not big enough to be a bloody nanny goat.'

George's only true diminutive friend (he stayed clear of his own size, as a rule) was a four-foot variety performer, Sadie Corré, a wonderful cat impersonator whom George had first met in a London Palladium pantomime, *Dick Whittington*.

One day Sadie suddenly asked him, 'Do you find that nurses *don't* look down on one? While most doctors treat us as 'patients', all the nurses I know have been angels'. George nodded, contemplating the many nurses he'd known in his past whilst a patient in hospitals throughout the world. He agreed that nurses were unique. 'But somehow', he used to say, 'I do not think they would like to be called angels.' He disliked that word's theatrical connotation.

In time, with hates and loves exaggerated at the end, he became obsessional about nurses and fondly related how a friend of his had served as a hospital orderly for many years; a short woman, she was perfectly formed in physique, although her height prevented her from becoming a state registered nurse. George's bitterness at such injustice grew to mammoth proportions in the last years of his life.

The first time George had ever been in a private hospital bed was in the Los Angeles Good Samaritan Hospital. His room had been thoughtfully furnished with a small dressing table and wardrobe, and the high surgical bed changed for one he could step into. He made no comment, but later when he was admitted to a hospital in Detroit he found himself requesting a low bed and an easily accessible wardrobe. Nurses were always told by George that all undersized patients feel better if no mention is ever made of the fact. 'It is a great "boost" to the morale if they are visited by senior members of the nursing staff.' He always apologized to those nurses who felt the raw edge of his tongue when he was impatient by explaining: 'We feel this impatience about *everything*; slow service in restaurants, lack of attention in shops, even the late delivery of newspapers. We always feel that, "They wouldn't dare to do this if we were bigger".'

George stayed in a large number of hospitals in his lifetime; in Sydney, in Rome, at the Burns Clinic in Michigan, and the Roosevelt Hospital in New York. In London, the Middlesex and University College Hospitals were just around the corner from his flat in Gordon Mansions, Bloomsbury, where he died, having earlier been to a hospital in Littlehampton, Sussex. There, he spent many hours over many days, being x-rayed and saying at the end of it, 'I can honestly say that I have never met a nurse of any creed, colour or position who did not make me feel a better person than I know myself to be'.

Towards the end, just before his final illness when I visited him at his flat, the Little Fellow made a toast, raising his glass of milk in the customary way (he'd been a lifelong teetotaller): 'To the diminutives of the future. Think of yourselves as being "normal", despite any loss of height or other disadvantages.' And to the so called 'normal' people he knew: ('You must not look down on us physically. If you do we shall look down on your often restricted mentality.' He once made an impassioned plea when he addressed a large group of London doctors and nurses. 'While you're about it,' he commanded, 'get the public to support your research into endocrinology. This is the principal hope for those who want to prevent babies being born with glandular anomalies; having to live with the handicap of restricted growth, we are compelled to live a schizophrenic existence.'

Wee Georgie Wood could do things on the stage that nobody else could. He utilized melodramatic sketches as though they were dramas of note. He'd turn on the pathos, milk it for all it was worth and then take his curtain call as gravely as did Wolfit in the more legitimate theatre, the difference being that George's call was self-mocking and gave way to a wealth of artistry and wit.

In his early years he liked people to speculate about his age and was, in fact, still youthful for his years – in his late seventies – until his first stroke. In his latter years he enjoyed being fêted, made an OBE and was delighted when Joan Miller and I celebrated his anniversary by taking a special dining room at the Savage Club to celebrate his eightieth with a birthday luncheon. Today in the Savage Club, where he was a miniature monument for half a century, his portrait still hangs on the bar walls, where his brother Savage members, holding their tankards, remember The Minute One, who never drank anything stronger than a glass of milk. Speeches were made at that last birthday by many, champagne toasts were drunk. The guest of honour drank milk.

Only those who knew him well realized how much his greatest asset as a star, his size, continued to rankle with him in his old age. He blamed 'the diminutive', as he called himself (hating the words 'midget' or 'dwarf'), for aborting his career as an actor of the Martin-Harvey type, who would have loved to play Sydney Carton in *The Only Way*. George Bernard Shaw uttered a half-truth when he told the music hall star that he would have made a good *King Lear*. In fact when George took a sublease of the Westminster Theatre in 1948, in order to bring Donald Wolfit back to the West End in my production of Ibsen's *The Master Builder*, it was not just a stunt. He liked to be associated with serious drama, his own amusing sketches had more than a hint of tragedy about them. A few years earlier still, he had presented John Steinbeck's play *The Moon Is Down* at London's Whitehall Theatre. If he was debarred by physique from playing in it himself, the next best way of compensation was to sponsor it for somebody else.

Despite his earnings in a lucratively successful career, he had very little in the bank when he died. His heart was cheered by an analytical yet deeply emotional mind, allied to a big spirit in a small physique. This furnished compensation of a kind.

'We never closed,' cried the Windmill, non-stop theatre during the war; yet it died before George Wood OBE did, the showman entertainer who never properly retired nor stopped being a colourful character.

Remembering Her . . .
A Tribute to Joan Miller 1910–1988

'Remember me when I am gone away' –
Christina Rossetti

Those who loved her – and to know her was to love her – were to lose an extraordinary spirit, and the theatre an actress of genius who was at the height of her powers in the post-war years. It was a terrible loss. One recalls Graham Greene's partiality to some lines of Browning to characterize his work: 'Our interest's on the dangerous edge of things; the honest thief, the tender murderer, the superstitious atheist. . . . Just when we are safest, there's a sunset touch. A fancy from a flower bell, someone's death, a chorus ending from Euripides. . . .'

17, Chesham Street,
London, S.W.1.
26th August, '45.

Dear Miss Miller,

May I take this opportunity of congratulating you upon your most moving performance as Rebecca in *Rosmersholm*? It was an exciting performance from every angle, and although I have no recollection of seeing you before, I shall count your acting in the powerful three-handed scene with Kroll and Rosmer, alongside that of Harold Scott as Vanya, Catherine Lacey as Jane Clegg and Wolfit as Lear – the three best acting performances of the last eighteen months.

In most little theatre schemes, the play is made to suffer by the frightful, rather 'precious' casting of the young actors and actresses who clutter up the stage, but rarely know how to cross it. For the first time in my life I have seen a first-rate play acted by a cast of actors, all of whom were well above the average. But in this group you succeeded in shining brighter than the rest. Thank you!

Yours very sincerely,
Peter Cotes

The Torch Theatre,
Wilton Place, S.W.1.
September 1, '45.

Dear Mr. Cotes,

Thank you for your most charming letter. I am glad you like *Rosmersholm* and my performance of Rebecca West. It is a wonderful play and a fine part.

I hope from my heart that something will develop from this first effort at the Torch. It is my dream to be a member of a group of experienced and talented people anxious to do good plays and to develop a virile type of acting. By some wonderful chance the six people in *Rosmersholm* have found that they can work together as a team in complete harmony and so their individual talents are heightened. I believe this harmony is essential for the play's sake and for the sake of the individual player.

Thank you again for writing to me,
Yours very sincerely,
Joan Miller

And that was how it all started. . . . Joan became in time my wife. Before that she had become the leading actress in a number of plays I directed and produced, mostly in our own theatre but sometimes in the West End.

Unfortunately the life of the little London Theatre Group, where I had first seen her, was short. That fine team of artists had to split and seek their bread and butter in the larger theatre. Still, I was to write at the time: 'Joan Miller and her colleagues had proved that working as a team could be done.' Three months after the Torch Theatre venture collapsed, Jon Godfrey died. As Joan Miller's husband he had been the force behind her in starting the group but had been in failing health for some time.

Determined not to give up the fight to prove that group theatre could work, Joan and I decided to enter into artistic partnership and searched London for suitable premises where we could put into practice much that we had learned in the theatre, as actor and director, respectively. We started our search in the winter of 1945, but it was April 1946 before the curtain rose on our first night.

Over many years Joan was to grow into simply the greatest actress I have ever known. As a partner, off-stage and on, she is beyond my powers of description. Her blazing vitality and complete truth made her unique. I need to write about her. Many people have suggested that I should. Yet, as my friend, the late Professor Morgan, academician and one time Warden of Toynbee Hall, once said, 'Certain modes of speech and fashions of proceedings should be excluded when discussing matters near the heart'. And yet, and yet – what Joan wrote (in the little poems found unexpectedly in a bottom drawer in the bedroom where I found her dead) came from the heart, and that's all that matters. She spoke the truth and her honesty and sensitive awareness remain more touching than any mere poetical technique. It was the humorist, Roger Woddis, who wrote that technique, like patriotism is not enough. Certainly, to divulge secrets that concern innermost feelings smacks of indecent exposure. To tell all, borders on exhibitionism, sometimes self-pity. So secrets of the heart had better remain so.

Genius is a much abused word. If ever an actress was touched by it, Joan was. The stage is no fairy-land, but she made it so, both as woman and as actress. By nature she was the most loving of women, to those who were close to her, the most devoted and heart-warming of friends. Through our struggles inside the theatre I was warmed by her presence at my side, forever exuding an inner strength. I loved her above all others, but maybe I failed to tell her so loudly, clearly and often enough.

After Joan had gone, I read some lines she had written when a young woman about her ambitions for the future. At the time, she had clearly not set forth on her trip to England, and her 'Testament' is interesting, as it was so nearly realized. Because of its self-explanatory nature and its 'timing' (something that as an actress she always strove to achieve) perhaps it is fitting to stand as an epitaph in her memory: *She never deviated as a woman or as an actress from doing what as a young girl she had set out to do.*

Testament of an Actress

I do not want to waste my life scrabbling for money during the day for the sole purpose of kicks in the evening. Acting, for me, is my kicks and my job, my enjoyment, my vocation, my work, rolled into one. Acting combines whatever artistic talent I have with pleasure, not just for myself, one hopes, but if successful, for other people. Perhaps the only reason for wanting to become an actor is that I feel in myself that acting is what I know I want to do.

Acting is not for me a whimsical glamour attraction. I have acted in enough amateur productions to have felt the strains, the downs, the difficulties, yet it is overcoming all these things that brings a satisfaction which is to be found in few places. I can see no end to learning and education in all forms as an actor; along with the intriguing balance of team-work and individuality, interest for me is always there. The team-work is being able to act with people and get on even outside the framework of the play, the individuality, being able to act at all.

I have a tremendous ambition for acting, and derive a tremendous amount of enjoyment from it. All aspects of acting fascinate me: study, rehearsal, character, performance, language, words, movement, text, friendship, people, life. This is all very well, but I have only taken this from acting having once found it. I did not go on the stage for the very first time because of these very fine-sounding ideas. My only reason for auditioning for a part in a play was to test my nerve. I was always nervous to do any form of public speaking. Having a strong interest in literature and the theatre, I thought if I could stand up in front of an audience in a play and not 'fluff' or break down, then I would conquer them for ever. I did just that and not only conquered the nerves but enjoyed the whole thing immensely. The more acting I did the more I got out of it, and even achieved a certain measure of success. From then on I knew acting was the thing I wanted to concentrate on, to improve myself and take it up as a profession, then to try and keep on improving.

*   *   *

Joan came here from Canada in 1934. Not a 'professional Canadian' (she never wore that country's badge as a mark of special distinction), she was above petty nationalism; an internationalist in feeling, she became a woman of the entire world. When she settled here in 1934, still in her early twenties, and despite later travelling in theatre to France, Holland, Australia and America, she never returned to her birthplace, Vancouver, feeling it too full of memories. . . .

She was one of two daughters; her sister, Dorothy, became a hospital nurse, later marrying a colonel in the Seaforth Highlanders. Dorothy and her husband, Ian Tait, died tragically young, within a few years of each other in the early 1950s. The nearest Joan ever got to going back to Canada was when we went to New York with *A Pin to See the Peepshow* in 1953 (nearly twenty years after she had left). By that time the urge to return was past, with her mother and sister both dead. Joan and her sister had been brought up single-handedly by a mother who was a matron in a hospital in British Columbia. This mother, Rhoda Tingle, had been deserted by her husband years before Joan wanted to leave for England, and so it was easy for Rhoda to accompany her here, ill though she was at the time.

For some years Joan had studied for the theatre in Vancouver, and she came to be regarded as Canada's foremost theatre actress. She used to say that such 'fame' was nothing much, because although Canada is a big country in size, there was at that time (the early thirties) only a tiny professional theatre existing throughout the continent, apart from English and American touring companies, who came for a season before they passed on. Eventually Joan left her home to try her luck in the professional theatre, having recently won the Bessborough Trophy as the Best Actress in Canada at the Dominion Drama Festival, held in Ottawa in 1934. The great critic and innovator, J.T. Grein, was the adjudicator, and heartened by his advice and enthusiasm, Joan made for England, accompanied by her terminally ill, ever doting mother. She came armed with letters of introduction, both from Grein and the Earl of Bessborough, the latter at the time Governor-General of Canada and whose trophy she had received for her performance as Elizabeth the Queen in Maxwell Anderson's play of the same name.

Several of the introductions bore some small fruit and Joan started by cutting her teeth in the West End as an understudy, sometimes covering those whose talents she by far outshone. Nevertheless, her principals, two of whom were Greer Garson and Vivien Leigh, went on to become world famous film stars. Joan never played for either of them except at understudy rehearsals. A principal she did deputize for was the already elderly Lady Tree, in the part of Mistress Quickly in Sydney Carroll's production of *Henry IV* (Part I). George Robey, the music-hall star was, as a production gimmick, playing Falstaff during its run at His Majesty's Theatre. (Later, Joan used to recall Lady Tree sending her wild flowers for her dressing room when her understudy went on. 'I cut them myself, straight from the garden', read her accompanying note of loving wishes.) Perhaps the older actress detected in the younger what could lay ahead. Many years later, following her West End début as an acknowledged star actress, I was to be told by Sydney Carroll that Joan was, in his eyes, always a *star* from the start.

Understudying Greer Garson in Laurence Olivier's very first production as a director, *Silver Arrow*, at the newly opened Whitehall Theatre, was a further period of marking time. Shortly after it closed Greer landed a Hollywood contract on the strength of being seen in the play. It was a first step towards *Mrs Miniver*.

Yet another job understudying; this time a complete unknown, who was making her first appearance on the professional stage in *The Mask of Virtue*. Vivien Leigh had just signed a contract with Alexander Korda, and consequently *The Mask of Virtue*, to be produced by Sydney Carroll at the Ambassadors Theatre, was being substantially backed by Korda's company, London Films. Vivien Leigh became, in time, an accomplished film actress, but when she started on the stage she had few clues about acting. In fact she had to be literally coached, sentence by sentence, by the young overseas actress, who already had a head start, through having played minor bits and pieces in the West End as a professional in the company of several seasoned performers. Sydney Carroll, a doyen of producers at that time, who had already engaged Joan previously for a part in *The Soldier's Fortune* at the Ambassadors, as well as Mistress Quickly, when he presented *Henry IV* (Part I), took the young understudy aside one day and whispered 'in confidence', (although everyone knew it!) that he had film company money behind his production. This West End engagement was, in reality, to help groom a new, inexperienced film star. 'My dear, we have to do *something* with this young woman. She's beautiful to look at, but devoid of any histrionic ability.' He looked at Joan knowingly. . . .

So it became the understudy's additional job, with marginally more experience than her principal, to teach the star to act. But beauty alone could not ensure a long run for the fledgeling's much publicized début, although the press was good for her looks and, due to tuition, she managed to keep the curtain up.

Despite having this background of amateur work in Canada, these several tiny West End engagements, and a season playing serving women and fairies in the Open Air Theatre in Regent's Park, the aspiring youngster was getting diverted in her profession. She had come to London to be a serious professional actress, because, from afar, it looked more promising than Vancouver did as a base. Now, months later, following her arrival, she found herself understudying others who were never off, except the already elderly Lady Tree. . . .

After looking around for further employment, (chiefly to provide additional support for her ill mother) Joan chanced upon a side-line. Every night after her stage performances, she appeared in cabaret; finally performing her own material in a solo sketch, *The Telephone Girl* at the Mayfair Hotel. At that time the Mayfair was an exclusive nitery where the main attractions were Ambrose and his Band and the Prince of Wales dancing with a new friend, Mrs Wallis Simpson. At one point in her engagement she was seen by the powers-that-be of early television, and invited to audition at the BBC's Alexandra Palace studios. Good looking, slender, and with obvious talent, she 'clicked' and was engaged on the spot. Subsequently she became the first personality to be thrown up by the infant TV, 'The very *first* star of television' as *The Times* was later to put it. Doubtless her cabaret persona in the *Telephone Girl* sketch gave the TV producers the idea that, as that character, the attractive young woman could interview famous names of the day; author J.B. Priestley, sculptor Jacob Epstein, cartoonist David Low, and a large number of others as well. It was a waste of her real talent, but it was work of a sort, with that additional income to help the mother who now increasingly depended upon her daughter's salary for her regular medical treatments. This was over a decade before the establishment of the NHS.

Thus Joan achieved fame, if not fortune, and became known to a growing public of early telly addicts as 'The Picture Page Girl'. The format of the programme broke new ground, as it was described in the *Daily Telegraph*:

> One of the star features of the BBC trial television programmes, which begin on Thursday from Alexandra Palace, is to be called 'Picture Page'. Mr. Cecil Madden, co-ordinating producer at the Palace, told me yesterday how this would be presented, and explained his experiments with the new technique of television.
>
> 'Picture Page' is a special pictorial version of the BBC magazine programme 'In Town Tonight'. It will be broadcast for the first time on Saturday, and afterwards once a week. Only the framework of the programme has yet been prepared. Its contents will be decided upon at the last minute.
>
> There will be no announcing in the usual way in this programme. Televiewers will see book-leaves turn over on the screen as the programme moves from one subject to another. Each page will dissolve into the picture of a telephone girl at a switch-board. She will be depicted watching a television screen, and will 'plug in' televiewers to the next item.
>
> The screen she is watching will then gradually enlarge to full size; showing the characters or the scene which she has mentioned.
>
> Miss Joan Miller, the young Canadian actress now appearing in *The Tiger* at the Embassy Theatre, will take the part of the telephone operator. The programme will last half an hour.
>
> L. Marsland Gander
29 Sept. 1936

There was even one occasion in 1939 when she made history: her face was transmitted from the Alexandra Palace Studio in

London to the Radio Corporation of America's station at River-head, New York. The distance covered was 3,000 miles. This was something scientists had believed impossible, as the maxi-mum range of television, up until that time, was considered to be approximately 25 miles. Over forty years later, Joan, in an interview, was to tell *The Times* in London on 17 April 1982: 'Of course it was a fluke, although according to some sections of the press I was the first television actress and the first human being to swim the Atlantic. Nobody knew how I had done it, I least of all!' However it became an event that the *New York Herald Tribune* on 2 January 1940 hailed as, 'More historic than Marconi's first signal from Cornwall to Newfoundland on 12 December 1901'. It was all disappointing and frustrating at the time however, and only incidental to what she had travelled here to do.

During the war years, with television studios closed, Joan was to get her first real continuous apprenticeship in England, play-ing in the Birmingham Alexandra Theatre Repertory Co. Here the company presented several seasons of prestigious plays, part-ly promoted by Joan's husband, Jon Godfrey. There she played with huge success such varied roles as Harriet Beecher Stowe (the anti-slavery campaigner), in Guy Bolton's *Hattie Stowe*,* Birdie in Lillian Hellman's *The Little Foxes*, The Tsarina in Osbert Sitwell's eponymous play, Mrs Dubedat in *The Doctor's Dilemma*, amongst others. She had always been fond of Bernard Shaw whilst growing up; now in England she was to play with distinction the Shavian repertoire: Eliza Doolittle opposite Esmé Percy in *Pygmalion*, Mrs George in *Getting Married* and Mrs Warren in *Mrs Warren's Profession*. In London, in the Festival of Britain's 1951 production of Shaw's *Candida*, her performance was counted by the renowned drama critic of *The Times*, A.V. Cook-man, as the finest of all the Candidas he had seen since the original, Janet Achurch, in 1904. It was not, however, until 1945, when she had returned to London from Birmingham, that she was spotted by the critic Desmond MacCarthy, who saw her as Rebecca West in Ibsen's *Rosmersholm*, at the tiny Torch

*Guy Bolton, collaborator and lifelong friend of P.G. Wodehouse, forged a link between Plum and me when I later negotiated TV rights for Wodehouse with the BBC.

Theatre in London. He praised her performance in lyrical fashion. The little production, despite its press, never transferred to a larger theatre.

I had read MacCarthy's piece in the *New Statesman* and went along to see this acclaimed young artiste. At that time, dabbling in many parts, I was writing a column as a guest drama critic for the old *Queen* magazine. I had seen already much quality acting in my life but now I realized that I had never before seen quite such exquisite playing. MacCarthy had described her as 'a beautiful Rebecca West, perhaps the best I shall ever see'. Others of lesser note followed his lead, and so I went along to see what the fuss was all about. Later, I gave it as my opinion in print:

> Well, here it is at last; a good play, one of Ibsen's best, with a most able body of actors, all of whom are intelligent enough to play as a team, but who gracefully allow the most important character to achieve the outstanding triumph. Miss Joan Miller, in the part of Rebecca, plays the most strong minded of all Ibsen's women like a tornado. This is the psychological study of the havoc wrought by excessive individualism. Many of the problems confronting those for whom Ibsen wrote are thought to be dated. But the mental conflicts between the sexes are as eternal as life itself. Miss Miller's acting moved me considerably more than did either of the two much publicised ladies who played *Hedda* a few years back to the thousands. The few hundreds who may have seen this present production of *Rosmersholm* should to my mind count themselves the more fortunate theatre-goers.
> 15 Sept. 1945

I was excited enough to write that fan letter, not something I have done very often.

What was not known to many people (except very occasionally to those actors who played alongside her) is the fact that from the time she came over here to make a career she was rarely free from physical pain. So much was wrong with her medically that it is now impossible to detail it all. It cast a shadow, one that she conquered and kept from ever becoming almighty. One of the wonders of Joan was her physical, as well as mental courage, in the teeth of the pain she bore for so many years in silence. Playing on, whilst tragically ill, debarred from acting, and finally confined to bed and armchair, she lived the last ten years of her life on borrowed time. Putting a brave face on it right to the end, she cooked a last meal before going to bed. . . .

In the pages that follow, I shall quote others who paid tribute at the memorial meeting held for her at the Royal Institute of International Affairs in St James's Square on Remembrance Day, 11 November 1988. It was a great feeling to see so many friends gathered together. Some of those present had travelled very long distances to remember Joan, the woman, others to pay respect to the actress who had brought so much pleasure to so many. Among the many who remembered Joan that day was Lord Goodman. Arnold Goodman is more adept than most of us at describing human feelings and steering them away from sentimentality, and was to say:

> . . . I have known Peter and Joan for upwards of 35 years and throughout the whole of that time although often separated by the different routes our lives took we have remained the firmest and most affectionate of friends. Originally we were brought together by a common almost passionate interest in theatre. I had no professional pretensions. My only performance on any stage was as the Dauphin in *St. Joan*, the school play, when the master concerned having seen me in rehearsal was anxious to cancel the entire performance. But with Peter and Joan I found a special delight in talking about theatre. They both of course enjoyed distinguished professional careers, but they also had a viewpoint which unlike many professionals was cultured, and perceptive and fair minded. Our friendship burgeoned from that very special interest into a mutual understanding respect and regard. I had a deep affection for them which I shall always retain.
>
> Their marriage was a legendary one, it breathed life and reality into the legal fiction that husband and wife are one. They lived for each other, and it is for that reason that all of us who are dear friends, must rally to Peter's support in the difficult days in front of him, before he comes to terms with

his loss and derives sufficient comfort from hallowed
recollections. Joan as a person was sheer delight, she was
kind and generous, and affectionate and always willing to
assist anyone in real need. She had a modesty which I
believe was a disadvantage to her professional career. I do
not think she ever realised how good she was. Although
there is no doubt about Peter's belief in her talent. She was
indeed in my judgement, which in these matters I can claim
to be not a bad judgement, a very great actress. I never saw
her give an unworthy performance, and I have vivid
recollections of her Constance in *King John* at Stratford, of
her Portia in *Julius Caesar* and of her Queen in *Cymbeline*. A
happy memory is escorting our greatest minister of the Arts,
Jennie Lee, to a performance of Eugene O'Neill's *A Touch of
the Poet* at Croydon. A most memorable performance. A part
that Joan also made her own was in *Woman in a Dressing
Gown*, when I saw her in a television presentation and where
with characteristic disregard for any material advantage she
elected to perform at Stratford-on-Avon, rather than to
appear in the film version of that play.

I believe Joan would have been established as one of the
great actresses of this generation, but for the advent of ill-
health and the blinkered nature of some of our commercial
managements. It was a privilege to have known her and like
everyone in this hall I shall retain the happiest and most
admiring of memories.

When Joan died, a number of poems were found in the proverbial bottom drawer. Some of them represent her strong
opinions about a variety of matters, others are light and amusing. At the memorial meeting, Yvonne Coullet read Joan's poem
Animal Think-Tank which was followed by John Westbrook's
stirring memory of her and then came tributes from fellow
actors, all of whom had worked with her: John Franklyn-
Robbins, Bonnie Hurren, Hugh Manning, Richard Bonneville,
Stephen Jenn, Hedli Niklaus and Eileen Atkins amongst others,
and my brother, Roy.

After our time together launching the New Lindsay Theatre,
which I have written about earlier, we found ourselves in demand by the commercial theatre, and it was *very* commercial.
From helping me run our own shows, Joan went into a play at

the Lyric, Hammersmith and on the strength of a good press, including a wonderful personal notice from Harold Hobson in *The Sunday Times*, the piece, *Dark Summer* by Wynyard Browne, transferred from the Lyric to the St Martin's in the West End. It was during our respective West End runs that we married: 'Well-known Actress Marries Theatrical Producer', ran the headlines of evening newspapers, over front-page pictures of our wedding. We were then unable to work together for a short time, while I directed Donald Wolfit in a revival of Ibsen's *The Master Builder* at the Westminster. After these productions we went up to Manchester together to renew our association as actress and director, running a permanent company at the Library Theatre. At the memorial meeting, our old friend from those Manchester days, Norman Swallow, recalled that time:

> It was sadly not very long ago while staying at a hotel in Manchester that over breakfast I learnt for the first time the sad news of dear Joan. I read it appropriately in the *Guardian*, the *Manchester Guardian*, as Joan and Peter and I would have called it. I also realised, there and then, that it was about a hundred yards from where I then was that I first met Joan and Peter. It was in the Queens Hotel that I first met them. The hotel has now been demolished and replaced with a rather tedious office block. I stood outside that block and began to reflect on those days when we were all together, approximately forty years ago. I then looked over across Manchester's Piccadilly, and there was another building, the old Broadcasting House which was where I had once worked.
>
> You can imagine how I felt on that morning, and I remembered meeting them both, and I also remember our first professional connection. It was a radio feature called I think, *The Play's the Thing*, (what else would it be called?) It was all about Peter's production in the Central Library Theatre, in Manchester, of a play by an American, Lee Gilbert, called *The Rising Wind*. The programme was a documentary about how the play was produced by Peter, and Joan played the leading part in it. The play was set in an American University, and Joan played the part of the wife of a professor and the theme was Un-American Activities. (American academics were being thrown out of

their universities at that time because of their so-called Un-American attitudes, it was the first play of its kind to be produced anywhere in the world.)

Almost in the same week I went with Joan to Leeds and she appeared in a radio play, that I produced and directed called, sounds unlikely really for Joan, *Lady Anne*. I think Lady Anne was called Lady Anne Clifford and she was a Yorkshire Lady, and the piece was set against a background of Cromwellian and Stuart Britain. When Peter was at the Library Theatre my wife Maidie and I went regularly. As I thought of Joan on that sad morning I remember thinking of all the plays that I had seen Joan in, all directed by Peter, brilliantly directed and marvellously played. I remember Ibsen's *John Gabriel Borkman*, I think of Strindberg's *Miss Julie*, I shouldn't perhaps say this was the part I most remember. She was absolutely magnificent. *A Pin to See the Peepshow*, I remember, *Candida* I remember. . . . I could go on and on.

I remember when we all moved to London at about the same time. I rather carelessly got a job in television and we had to come to London, we kept up with Joan and Peter; they were among our closest friends. Always marvellous. And if you ever wanted to talk about any subject whatsoever, however delicate, or important, or emotional you could always talk to Joan about it and she would respond.

I remember the known and unknown actors and actresses who spoke from the platform that day. They spoke movingly about the woman they had acted with; some of them read her little verses, those odds and ends mentioned earlier, written during those last months of her life, in her by then shaky hand. She had suffered the first of many heart attacks, (the final one taking her away) while playing Amanda in a highly successful revival of *The Glass Menagerie* at Liverpool which was scheduled for West End production. The various tributes were touching and should not go unrecorded.

In the case of one of them, John Westbrook, he was to leave the world only a few months later. Beryl Westbrook, his widow, found John's notes for his memory of Joan and I can do no better than publish a letter she has generously given me permission to print in its entirety.

Thank you so much for your letter. I know John gave a great deal of thought to his tribute to Joan. In his desk were fortunately found the notes he had prepared. I have assembled these and send them now by proxy . . .

John used to say he had seen only two great performances in his life in the theatre and one of these was by Joan in *A Pin to See the Peepshow*. He had supported her, playing a minute role in the production, before becoming one of the leading 'voices' on radio, after which time he left the theatre for the microphone.

Over our thirty-one years of marriage he spoke of Joan's performance many, many times. He watched it from the wings every night. Her great cries as she was taken out of her cell to her death were something he'd never forget. He even went so far as to write her a 'fan' letter and was much touched by her simple unassuming reply – from this great actress to a young actor just starting out in the theatre. . . .

John Westbrook also read several of Joan's poems. As one of the best readers of verse in the country it was no surprise that he spoke them so well.

Hedli Niklaus, nowadays a prominent radio actress, was another who recalled the part Joan had played in her life.

When Joan and Peter came to stay it was as exciting as Christmas. I knew they were special to my mother, who had written a book with Peter on Charlie Chaplin and who loved to watch Joan perform over and over again. So we would turn the house upside down to make sure everything was perfect for them. Their arrival was never disappointing. They would sweep in, bringing with them all the excitement and glamour of the 'other' world of the theatre. I would watch and listen, fascinated, and spend secret moments in the bathroom trying to look like Joan in the bathroom mirror (I can still do it.)

For me then, and later, Joannie was everything an actress should be: deep-voiced, perfumed, expansive and passionate. She introduced me to Beauty Without Cruelty, told me it was never too early to look after my skin, and more importantly showed me the other side of theatre, the hard work behind the magic moments. She never talked down to me, which I greatly prized, and her fierce commitment and articulacy illuminated what she had to say, and forced me to think through all sorts of issues, often uncomfortable ones. She and Peter were also responsible for introducing me to the glories of the 'cold collation', which up to that point had been quite outside the scope of my experience.

Some years later, in my teens, I helped Joan and Peter during one of their house moves. However busy we were we always stopped for a drink at the end of the day. I can see Joannie now, sitting straight-backed in her chair, the greens and golds she loved so much bathed in the soft glow of the lights. She would look at me over the top of her reading glasses, rather fiercely, her cheeks slightly flushed, and then we started talking, debating, arguing. There was no question of giving her anything but the full measure she gave you, and it was exhilarating, rather like a roller coaster ride. Joan's humour was dark, ironic rather than facetious. She saw the world as it was with all its short-comings, and found confirmation of people's inadequacies wryly and sadly predictable.

I find her easy to remember. She was part of my childhood and developing self. She was a magnificent role-model with her physical bravery and toughness of spirit combined within a deeply loving nature. I was so lucky to have known her.

Completing her memory, Hedli read Joan's *Our Cleaning Lady*. The character of the cleaner was based upon a splendid lady, Mrs O'Hara, who worked in that capacity for much of our married life. Since Hedli remembered our 'daily help' from her own visits to stay with us down the years, it was right that she should speak Joan's lines about another good friend who is, today, no longer with us. Although *Our Cleaning Lady* was based upon Mrs O'Hara, the latter's character was totally dissimilar to the Lady in the poem, an inhabitant of the Oxfordshire country-side!

Hugh Manning, a sterling actor and friend, a one-time president of British Actors Equity, remembered Joan and touched upon an aspect of the woman and actress when he recalled first memories.

My first memory of Joan was across the footlights. Yes, there were footlights on the stage in the 1940s! She was a member of Derek Salberg's Repertory Company at the Alexandra Theatre, Birmingham and with the power and sensitivity of her performances, she made a great impression on an aspiring young actor.

Later on, in 1947 she came to see *Twelfth Night* at the Open Air Theatre in Regent's Park in which I played Antonio. She was considering playing Queen Elizabeth in *The Imperial Votaress*, a play by Sydney Carroll, and she asked me to rehearse some scenes of the play with her with a view to its presentation in the West End. We had a week of intensive rehearsals and I have a lasting memory of the encouragement and strength she gave to me then.

She was an actress of wide emotional range and she could be strong and at the same time sensitive and vulnerable, and it is sad that the long illness she endured and which caused her so much pain limited her appearances and prevented her taking her rightful place among other great actresses of the day. My friend, Kenneth Tynan, considered her to be one of our finest actresses.

I kept in touch with her at lengthy intervals until a few months before she died, and remember her personally for the kindness and consideration she always displayed on these occasions and for the love and loyalty she gave to Peter which was so well known to all their friends.

Towards the end of her life, when a confirmed invalid, Joan took to guiding those aspiring protégés in whom she had confidence. One of the many young folk she helped in the 1980s was Richard Bonneville, now, in the 1990s a leading actor at Stratford-on-Avon; he went to Joan for advice and stayed to benefit from that first meeting. He, too, spoke of her as his mentor, like so many actors who came that day to celebrate her life.

I met Joan in the summer of 1985, shortly before I went to the Webber Douglas Academy. I would visit once a week and over tea and biscuits would try and tease from her stories about her illustrious career. She would have none of it. Instead she would brandish the play we had chosen to work on that week and would I please turn to Act Two.

One play she loved was Shaw's *The Doctor's Dilemma*. And one passage in particular we would read aloud over and over, her index finger often halting me in mid-sentence: 'Your breathing is poor, your phrasing, worse. Again, please.'

The artist Louis Dubedat is dying. In attendance are his doctors and, most importantly, his beloved wife, Jennifer.

Richard Bonneville then read Dubedat's last speech. A death scene this may be but Joan held this to be Shaw's affirmation of life!

Bonnie Hurren, actress of experience and charm, no stranger to both of us as a friend, read also. Bonnie had been with Joan in the try-out of a Dostoevsky play, *Mistress of Mordazov*, retitled as a comedy for the stage, *My Uncle's Dream*. But before she read Joan's little verse on Dorothy Parker, she too, was to remember their association as actresses.

My own strongest feeling about Joan was that she was a person who 'made a difference' – who touched and changed or influenced many lives in a personal and profound way. She had time for me when I needed it – even though she herself must have been struggling with her own frustrations (during rehearsals for *Uncle's Dream*). She had a generosity of spirit and kindness that is very, very rare in the theatre, or in life! and was in the best possible way one of life's special people. All this quite apart from, and yet obviously a part of, her great talent as an actress.

Then there were those present who remembered without reading verse. Stephen Jenn played a leading role in *Gigi* opposite Joan. He benefited from the experience of playing with her and attempted to mount a production of the play *Harold and Maude* for the West End. He planned that Joan would have played the part that Madeleine Reynaud had created in a Paris production of the same play.

I recall Joan instantly both on and off stage in words such as 'truth' and 'mean it' and 'reality'. Also I regret not having managed to mount *Harold and Maude* for her, as I know there will come a time when producers say 'Yes now is right!' and then clamour for it. I think she saw, and certainly I saw, something of Joan in Maude. Towards the end of the play the two have an exchange.

HAROLD: Maude, please, Don't die, I couldn't bear it. Please don't die.
MAUDE: But Harold, we begin to die as soon as we are born. What is so strange about death? It's no surprise. It's part of life. It's change.

Joan, from our appearance together in *Gigi* challenged me to always strive to make it absolutely truthful. She actually made any actor, I think, feel they had to earn their right to be on a stage. And she was such fun!

Joan had been so intensely concerned about the anti-apartheid problem that it was natural to ask the black actor Louis Mahony to read pieces she had written about both Soweto and Nelson Mandela. That foremost victim of miscarriage of justice had not then been released, hence Joan's poem in dedication, titled simply *For Nelson Mandela*.

On the platform, also, was John Franklyn-Robbins, for years an actor of distinction and rare versatility who had been with Joan on stage in *The Man* and on screen in *The Haven*. He gave his impressions of seeing and observing her courage, as well as acting styles, in the different performances she had given. John had been youthful at the time and was keenly observant, anxious to learn and again talked about the kindness extended to him by the actress who was to remain in his memory so many years later. Then, as an unknown (later he was to be one of the leading players at the National Theatre), both shy and curious, he watched from the sidelines, the backstage wings and the studio floor. He referred to her as a 'warrior' who just happened to be a very great actress indeed.

Joan had also been one of the leading players in the 1957 season of Shakespeare at Stratford-on-Avon. Eileen Atkins, one of today's finest players, and a great favourite, paid her respects to the woman whose train she had carried some thirty years earlier in *Cymbeline*.

I was very impressed by the fact that she spoke as an equal with us 'walk-ons', her ladies in waiting in *Cymbeline*; this was unusual in those days, the star didn't really talk to the riff-raff. I remember that she listened to what we said and that she was very concerned that I had to wear a very heavy dress and with no air-conditioning it was very hot. She always remembered little things that we told her and in no way acted as the star she certainly was. I don't remember seeing her angry or cross ever, except on someone else's behalf.

I wish I'd known her better because clearly she was a very remarkable woman.

This tribute from one artistc to another was followed by Eileen reading one of Joan's favourite poems by Christina Rossetti which fittingly brought this celebration of Joan's life to an end:

> Remember me when I am gone away,
> Gone far away into the silent land . . .

*   *   *

I started this memoir of Joan Miller with a prologue concerning our first meeting – an exchange of correspondence contained in my fan letter to her and the response it drew. It would not, perhaps, be out of order, therefore, if I allowed our curtain to descend upon one of the last letters my Joan ever wrote to me. It was on the occasion of our Ruby Wedding and the letter was headed:

May 19 1948   –   May 19 1988

40 YEARS ON

We've done it – we've done it!
We've lived the long years through – side by side.
My darling – My husband – My Friend – My Love
My everything in the world.

Thank you for your courage –
Thank you for your never-ending help and patience –
Thank you for your friendship, your comradeship.
Thank you for giving me one human being in whom I could

completely trust and rely upon.
Thank you above all for your love and for *you*.

I love you in such an enlarged way that I cannot describe it,

I can only thank you forever and always from your love –
your wife – your Babe – your Old Girl

She was to die less than four months later. . . . Excessively sentimental you may think – but, in the circumstances, perhaps, that's not such a bad thing after all.

> Woman much missed, how you call to me, call to me
>   saying that now you are not as you were
> when you had changed from the one who was all to me
>   but as at first, when our day was fair.
> From The Voice by Thomas Hardy
> (Love Poems, 1912)

Appendix 1

Theatre Directing Career (own productions included)

An Inspector Calls
Angel Street (Gaslight)
The Animal Kingdom
Anna Christie
Back to Methuselah
The Biggest Thief in Town
Birdcage
Book of the Month
Border Incident
Call on the Widow
Candida
The Cardinal
Caste
The Children's Hour
Christmas Tree
Come Back Little Sheba
Epitaph for George Dillon
Everybody Cheer
The Father
Finishing School
For Services Rendered
Girl on the Highway
Happy and Glorious
Happy Holiday
Hamlet
Hidden Stranger
Home of the Brave
Hot Summer Night
The Impossible Years
Janie Jackson
John Gabriel Borkman
Lady Godiva
Land of the Living

Loaves and Fishes
The Long Mirror
Look No Hands
Loss of Roses
The Man
The Man Who Changed His Name
The Master Builder
Mid-Channel
Miss Julie
Mountain Fire
The Mousetrap
Mrs Basil Farringdon
The Odd Ones
The Old Ladies
Paint Myself Black
Pick-Up Girl
A Pin to See the Peepshow
Rainbow
Ridgeway's Funfair
The Rising Wind
Rocket to the Moon
The Rope Dancers
So Wise So Young
Squaring the Circle
Staring at the Sun
There's Always Juliet
Tom Pike
Village Wooing
Walk Into My Parlour
What Goes Up
What the Public Wants
Youth at the Helm

Film and TV Productions – UK and Abroad

Area Nine
Ashes in the Wind
Candida
The Father
Favonia
The Haven
The Hungry God
The Infinite Shoeblack
The Invaders
The Inward Eye
Jane Clegg
Lady Must Sell
Long Distance
Look in Any Window
The Macropolus Secret
The Mask
Master of Music
No Other Wine

Not Proven
The Offence
The Rehearsal: Before & After
The Right Person
The Same Sky
Shadow of the Vine
Suspect
The Terror
Tigress on the Hearth
What the Public Wants
When Men and Mountains Meet
Wild Justice
Winter in Ischia
Woman in a Dressing Gown
World of Wooster
Yesterday's Mail
The Young and the Guilty

Acting Career – Theatre and Film

Accident
Alibi
Anne One Hundred
Beware of Pity
Birdcage
Bow Bells
The Breadwinner
Caravan
Carnival
Cavalcade
Charlot's Non-Stop Revue
The Circle
Consider Your Verdict
Don't Take it to Heart
Faces
Fingers
The Flag Lieutenant
Flying Colours
The Gentle Sex
Golden Boy
Good Night Vienna
The Great God Brown
The Hand of the Potter
Hearts Are Trumps
Henry V
Her First Affaire
Hindle Wakes
I See a Dark Stranger
In the Duchess's Arms
Kipps

The Last Stone
The Little Damozel
Mr Penny's Tuppence
Mr Pimpernel Smith
A Murder Has Been Arranged
The One Girl
The Other Woman
Pal O'Mine
Pastor Hall
Peter Pan
Pilgrim's Way
The Rake's Progress
The Red Dog
Rise Above It
Small Hotel
Spring's Awakening
Staalag 17
Susie
This Happy Breed
Thunder Rock
To Kill a Cat
Tomorrow's Eden
Tomorrow's Sun
The Ugly Duchess
The Upturned Glass
What the Public Wants
The Way to the Stars
While Parents Sleep
The Windmill Man

Appendix 2

Peter Pan

Sheila Johnston subsequently wrote an article on the Steven Spielberg film production:

J.M. Barrie's 1904 play *Peter Pan* exhorted us to 'clap if you believe in fairies'. One wonders what response that line would get from today's cynical audiences, but it certainly wouldn't be a standing ovation. Still, while the story and all it stands for may have gently gathered cobwebs, if anyone can update it and sell it to modern, Ninja Turtle-touting kids, it will be Steven Spielberg, the movie-brat who, many reckon, never grew up and who has now filmed the classic fantasy as *Hook.* . . .

It will be intriguing to see how Barrie's whimsical vision will be transformed, but one thing is clear; the resemblance to the original story will be very approximate. 'We didn't even read the book first – you do just have to assume it's a very different script.'

The Independent
6 September 1991

But 'not having read the book first' did not prevent the makers of *Hook* from saying in *The Observer* how much they admired and loved Peter Pan! The piece by Richard Brooks went on to say that Spielberg 'has an unsurpassed ability to make movies that capture the hearts and minds of the young. . . . He has the knack of rediscovering lost youth on celluloid. Making *Hook* was a chance for him to "root" for his child-hood hero, Peter Pan'.

Appendix 3

Roger Moore article from *Plays and Players*

One Night on Broadway

Playgoers must often wonder why productions which are generously praised by critics after their first nights are sometimes withdrawn almost immediately. The story of the Broadway production of A PIN TO SEE THE PEEPSHOW, which suffered precisely this fate, is told here by Roger Moore who played a leading part in it. He was fortunate himself in that the production led to a film contract with M-G-M and a leading role in Noel Coward's THIS HAPPY BREED on American TV. He last appeared in the West End in I CAPTURE THE CASTLE two years ago.

**by
Roger
Moore**

WHEN I was a drama student, I once passed Anton Walbrook strolling conspicuously along Charing Cross Road. How wonderful it must be, I thought, to be so easily recognised in the busiest street—even when wearing large dark glasses. I just couldn't wait to be in the same happy position myself.

So when the eve of my first West End appearance arrived, and I was beginning to think that the chance of impressing myself indelibly in the public memory had finally arrived, you can imagine my fury on learning that I was to wear, by arrangement with Max Berman, a huge 19th century gendarme's hat that would completely hide my face.

Behind a Chinese Helmet

On my second London appearance I played a Chinese Officer of the Guard, and again, by arrangement with Max Berman, my features were deliberately concealed—this time by an enormous brass helmet.

Years passed, most of them in repertory or as an understudy, so that the West End public should never see me at all, until I found myself about to make my debut on Broadway. The British public had been spared even the tiniest glimpse of me, but the Americans were going to have their fill. Fame was to be mine at last, and whenever I walked through the teeming streets of New York people would turn to stare at me in wonder. Or so I thought. . . .

If you care to turn up the record of that production in an American theatre annual for the 1953-54 season you will find: *A Pin to See the Peepshow*, followed by the names of the authors, the director, the producer, the stars and other players, and—in the smallest type of all—"Opened September 17, closed after one performance".

To anyone except the 20-odd people like myself who were concerned in the production, *A Pin to See the Peepshow* must seem to have been the biggest flop of all Times Square. And the people who had seen the play produced in London at the Bolton's

Theatre and knew that only the interference of the Lord Chamberlain prevented its transferring into the West End, must have felt there was a story behind the fiasco.

There *was* a story—one of the craziest in the crazy world of the theatre.

I came into it by being offered two plays. The first I turned down because I didn't like the play and felt sure it could not run. The second was *A Pin to See a Peepshow*, which attracted me because it was to be directed by Peter Cotes, with his wife, Joan Miller, whom I have always considered our best dramatic actress, as leading lady. This was the partnership that had scored such a success with the play in London.

We opened "cold" (without the usual provincial tour) at the Playhouse Theatre, New York, on September 17, after three well-received public dress-rehearsals. It was a tremendously successful first night, and we were told in our dressing-rooms afterwards by enthusiastic people who had seen the show, including Hermione Gingold and Oscar Hammerstein, that we had a sure hit.

Honoured at Sardi's

At Sardi's, later that evening, all the distinguished diners rose to their feet and applauded Joan Miller as she walked in—an honour that at that time was still reserved for a handful of Broadway's finest stars. And in the early hours of the next day we trooped hopefully to Times Square to read the notices in the morning papers.

Now the New York critics are notoriously trenchant, always liable to write such killing quips as: "The X—— Y—— opened on Broadway last night. Why?" And the title of our play was a crying invitation to be vitriolic. But there was not a disapproving note. The play, the production and the players were praised most generously. Joan Miller's own performance was hailed in such terms that *A Pin to See the Peepshow* might have been expected to run on the strength of that alone.

So I spent a lazy, blissfully happy day, arriving at the theatre in the evening

ROGER MOORE: *"I wanted to be recognised by theatregoers whenever I walked along the street."*

expecting to find an excited company congratulating one another on their success. They were certainly excited, but not in the way I had imagined. For on the notice board was pinned a brief, fatal note to the effect that the play had closed.

Despondently, and utterly defeated, I collected my almost virgin sticks of Five and Nine make-up, threw them into a hold-all with the rather splendid socks I had bought for the show, and left the theatre. Instead of battling through the 13 scenes of our theatrical epic on the Bywaters murder case, in which I was nightly to murder a husband, see my mistress hanged and then hang myself, I slunk away to the Roxy Cinema to see the birth of CinemaScope with *The Robe*. And as I watched the batches of Christians being thrown to the lions in glorious Technicolor for the amusement of Caligula, I thought of myself and my fellow-actors at the mercy of Broadway vagaries and our producer.

No Wall Street Debut

It was unfortunate for us that this producer (the American equivalent to the English management) was making her Broadway debut too. It was positively fatal that she had *never* made her Wall Street debut.

On the day we opened we had to borrow 500 dollars in order to get the curtain up at all. And when, the morning after the premiere, there was less than a 100 dollars in advance bookings at the box-office, the whole situation became hopeless.

Our trouble had been that this producer evidently believed that no news was good news, in so far as there seemed to be no publicity whatsoever, prior to opening. Not even the most golden of "rave" notices could prevail after this.

All that remained for me of this opportunity to become famous was to collect the two weeks salary that American Equity rules shall be deposited with them for each actor in any new production. With this in my pocket, I was thrown out on to the streets of New York, where not a single passer-by was ever likely to stare at me as, years before, I had stared enviously at Anton Walbrook in Charing Cross Road. And *I wasn't* hiding behind large dark glasses.

WORKING FOR SUCCESS: Peter Cotes watching Joan Miller rehearse with Roger Moore for his ill-fated production of A Pin to See the Peepshow at New York's Playhouse Theatre in 1953. This same team will work together again on television next month in The Invaders. *Photo: New York Times*

Appendix 4

Letter from Kenneth Tynan to Joan Miller

19 Upper Berkeley St.
W. 1.

10th June 1951

Dear Miss Miller;

Taking your first curtain call after the last performance of "Peepshow" on Sunday night, you may have heard a pretty hysterical voice roaring "Bravo!" I was finding it very difficult to applaud anyway; it seemed like the most callous kind of irreverence; but there was a tumult going on inside me which had to be let loose. So, in a strange, possessed way, I shouted my thanks.

No performance in my memory has broken down so many of the barriers that hide the last, deepest wrath of the human heart. Your incoherent battle with the hypodermic in the penultimate scene was not merely a sordid entreaty; it had the horrid anger of a child, awaking from its first nightmare, the rawness and the fright we feel when we see and touch inevitability. I have never been so appallingly convinced that the bottom of my stomach was going to drop out. The "hospital" feeling, the first examination feeling — that sense of the unalterable — has never been so violently conveyed to me.

My wife and I, normally a gay enough

193

pair of cynics, cried in the taxi home. It may be that the fact that Pepshaw is recent history made it seem more ominous and awful; as Brecht has found in Germany, a lot of stories become more effective if the audience knows the ending, and becomes absorbed by how things happen, rather than by *what* things happen; whatever it was, we had seen the clearest most moving piece of acting in London, and we both knew we would never have the courage to see it again.

I shall be grateful if you can find a moment to tell your husband what delight I took in his production — especially in the party scene (Scene 2) and the magnificently clumsy, casual, and cold-blooded handling of the last scene of all.

In every generation there are about half a dozen actresses who are always better than their scripts: and actresses like this deserve and need plays to be written for them. Their skills demand vehicles. For me, at this moment, you are one of these; and, eliminating perhaps some of the over-florid and pompous gush in this letter, I intend to hang on to that opinion for at least twenty years.

Again, many thanks:

Yours sincerely

Ken Tynan.

Appendix 5

Afterthoughts on *The Biggest Thief in Town*

The Biggest Thief in Town, by the American blacklisted writer, Dalton Trumbo, played, during its run, at three London theatres and had in the course of its career four different star actors in the title role. A record?

The trouble started when 'Thief' number one, Hartley Power, had to leave the cast early in its West End run (it had transferred from the New Boltons to the Duchess theatre). He had to honour a contract he'd signed prior to signing the one with me for the Boltons run. This came as quite a surprise to me for there is always a likelihood, when one has a potential winner, that through its success outside the West End it will be offered a transfer into the West End itself. The story of *Pick-Up Girl* needs no re-telling here, and other banned plays such as *The Children's Hour* and *A Pin to See the Peepshow* were offered transfers during their New Boltons theatre runs, which I was unable to accept owing to the Lord Chamberlain's ruling. *The Biggest Thief in Town* also risked the Censor's ban at one stage in its life; cuts were to be made before I took it into the West End. In this case, the threat was not pursued.

The Biggest Thief in Town was Hartley Power's biggest break since he came to England from America in the 1920s in a show called *Broadway* at the old Adelphi in the Strand. He was getting sole star billing, with me, over the title, something that he'd never achieved before (although he had co-starred with Yoland Donlan, understudy to Judy Holliday – herself unknown at the time – in Laurence Olivier's production of *Born Yesterday* at the Garrick). I was shocked when I heard the news, shortly after the run had started at the Duchess, that Power would have to leave the cast within the next six weeks, less than two months after its opening. He was crestfallen too, but as he had another show to go into, like most actors he was living for the present. So I promptly set about finding another 'Thief' to take his place when he left the play for a comparatively small part in a Drury Lane spectacular, *South Pacific* by Rodgers and Hammerstein, starring Mary Martin. That, of course, ran a long time but never again in his lifetime did Hartley Power get such a big chance as the one he had to leave so early in its run.

With the show still playing to full houses it seemed stupid to with-draw the piece when the rest of the more than competent company shone in a production that was being so enthusiastically received. In the belief that no one actor is completely indispensable – although I have seen many good actors make bad plays better by their expertise – and believing in the play as a superb farce (a belief that the critics had endorsed to a man), I cabled the author's agent in New York, asking her to sound Trumbo about ideas for a replacement. It needed to be a good American actor who could come across immediately. Trumbo, at the time a refugee from Senator McCarthy's notorious House Un-American Activities Committee, promptly suggested the one-time group theatre actor, J. Edward Bromberg, then a well known Hollywood feature player. That was how 'Joe' Bromberg came to appear in his first – and last – London production.

The actor, good in straight parts as I was later to learn, was no dab hand in farce. He had, after all, been working with such method directors as Lee Strasberg and Harold Clurman for most of his career on stage. He had also appeared in countless Trumbo scripted films in Hollywood and had been well regarded, until, as a known politico, he had been summoned to return from the West Coast to the East and give evidence before the House Un-American Activities Committee, then busily 'blacklisting' artists of all types. The hearings were a mockery, careers were wrecked overnight unless the victims were like Arthur Miller or Lillian Hellman, two of those who refused to name names and break down under the threat of imprisonment. Having been a communist, or even having liberal feelings or associations, was enough for artists to find themselves out of work for good. Trumbo, a victim, had himself appeared and fled to Mexico immediately afterwards, with his successful screen writing career in Hollywood in complete tatters. His one stage play, *The Biggest Thief in Town*, had been produced on Broadway at the heart of the crises and despite having a star in the title role, had opened and closed within a week.

I was shocked by the first sight of Bromberg when he got off the ship from America. He was clearly a very sick man. It was the first time I'd ever gone in for blind booking of a leading role. I'd not seen the actor perform on stage and when rehearsals started, I realized that although he'd always given a good account of himself in films (I'd seen a few of them) he was a vastly different actor on stage. Film performances are often made by imaginative directing and editing, musical effects, and all the other factors inserted when a film is being cut and dubbed after the director has shot his sequences in a certain way. Whereas in the theatre, once the curtain's up, the actor is out there on his own after, admittedly, much longer periods of rehearsal than he ever gets in films. But certain roles, however well written, may have to be carried by the actors.

Liam Redmond, a good if not startling actor, but only a limited comedian, had filled in for Hartley after his departure for the big-time musical. He had bridged the gap and continued the run until the time when Bromberg's visa and US passport clearance were both in order for him to come across to accept work away from the USA.

When I first saw Joe it became apparent to me why his travel had been delayed and he couldn't fly. His heart trouble – he had had a number of heart attacks through his ordeal while appearing as an 'unfriendly witness' – had not been disclosed to me, despite the common knowledge in America of the trials and tribulations he'd suffered at McCarthy's hands. And now with my first 'Thief' in a musical and my second 'Thief' on only a limited run contract, my third 'Thief' seemed only barely alive to take over this long and exhausting role.

Joe was a shocking mud colour, perspiring, short of breath and on heavy medication. While one could only sympathize with his wish to leave the US after his grilling and subsequent persecution, and with every door to work closed to him, it was nevertheless reckless of those who'd known the poor chap's state of mind and heart before he made the journey. Apart from anything else they were sacrificing a play's run and a cast's livelihood by such a recommendation. The part of the Undertaker was the linchpin of the piece, the actor virtually never off-stage during the play's action. Although to date the run had been successful, it still needed to consolidate itself. Two changes already was no way to give even the most 'worked-in' (which it wasn't) production an even chance.

As it was, the outcome to the whole tragic engagement was that shortly after he'd opened, poor Joe Bromberg was discovered dead in bed from a cardiac arrest. He was found by the housekeeper of the small Earls Court hotel where he was living during his stay, and I was quickly summoned to identify the body. I cabled Joe's wife in Los Angeles at once and made arrangements for her to take a plane flight to come across immediately.

I posted the closure notice on the backstage call-board the same night as the understudy from the stage management was appearing bravely for the dead principal during the few performances left until the end of the week. It was a terrible shock for all who had known the actor, who had started to feel his feet by getting a grip on his role, that after appearing for so few performances in the title-role he was no longer there. It was a shame, too, that a show which had started out so well should have ended so sadly.

However, there were still signs – even with an understudy deputizing, that the production might survive – and I gambled with the idea of retaining the current cast intact and soldiering on, albeit at another (the third) theatre. I looked around for yet a fourth 'Thief' and it was, I suppose, natural that I chose the Canadian actor, Bernard Braden. He had played very successfully for me in the thriller, *The Man*, which I'd directed for a goodish run at first Her Majesty's and later the St Martin's in the West End. Braden had co-starred opposite Joan Miller in that production and, although it was a tingling thriller and he had formerly been thought of more as a light entertainer than a straight actor, he'd acquitted himself well. Now, I thought, Bernie could revert to natural comedy again and that's how he played the 'Thief', the fourth star actor to play it in a row. I'd managed to get the tiny Fortune Theatre, then 'dark', and we opened again only one month after we'd closed at the Duchess. My original production was intact, except that Braden played the Undertaker with an American accent, which leaned heavily on his native born Canadian.

Well, that made a total of four 'Thieves' in a six-month run and despite the choppings and changing the production still held up, coming across as a very funny farce – and not, as Lillian Hellman told me it had been on Broadway, 'a socially conscious comedy; here it was a plain uproarious farce – there, when seen in America (where it ran four nights only on Broadway) it was a "straight" play instead of a farce'. Lillian, whose *The Children's Hour* I had directed at the New Boltons (with Joan Miller, David Markham, Mary Merrall and Jessica Spencer), saw the West End production of *The Biggest Thief in Town*, as well as the Broadway one, and felt that there was no comparison as to which was the better. She attributed its run in London to the fact that it had been directed as farce, *as written* by the author. This was high praise indeed from one noted for being a tough lady.

At the Fortune, certainly, the play still had mileage, but as transfers invariably affect the smooth running of any production, it finally exhausted what now became a limited public. If we had continued as we opened, with the original cast and production, I feel that it might have run for ever. . . .

Appendix 6

First sighting of *The Mousetrap*

I first heard from Peter Saunders in a letter dated 29.2.52, from his office in Trafalgar Square. He asked if I'd care to read *The Mousetrap* by Agatha Christie which, as I knew, Attenborough was doing, playing the part of Sgt. Trotter. He went on to say how much he'd like to meet me after I'd read it in order to have my observations on it, and concluded by congratulating me on the success of the recently produced *The Biggest Thief in Town* in the West End. This he confessed to having enjoyed 'so much'.

I replied on 3.3.52, acknowledging the script and agreeing that a meeting might be a good idea. To this letter Saunders replied on 5.3.52, to say that if I was free on the following Saturday morning, we could perhaps meet at about noon for a chat in his office, followed by lunch. A short time later I replied: 'perhaps your secretary will ring through to me at the Saville Theatre stage door where I am at the moment rehearsing a new production, letting me know where you propose lunching and I can then come on to you when the morning rehearsal ends at 1.o'c.'

Saunders personally got smartly on to the phone and advised me that he'd book a table at the Carlton Hotel for one o'clock, and that he greatly looked forward to our meeting then.

And so we met. . . .

Appendix 7

'And so it goes on . . . and on'

Peter Saunders is still going merrily on ('And so it goes on and on – and on!' Harold Pinter once wrote to me on a postcard, but whether he was referring to the play or its manager I have no idea), and in *The Daily Telegraph*, dated 20 November 1992, he was reported as saying:

> 'After the first performance we sat up until three or four in the morning talking about it and Agatha Christie said, "It's my fault, I haven't written enough laughs for a comedy-thriller and I've written too many for a whodunnit."
>
> 'I looked at Dickie because actors don't usually like laughs being taken out and I said, "Would you mind if we removed the laughs that affect the tension," and he said, "Not a bit." So we went through the whole script and took out six or seven laughs and the next day the play was completely different.'

I replied to the same paper:
24 Nov. 1992

The Manager of *The Mousetrap* paints for your correspondent, Charles Spencer, a fanciful picture of that play's beginnings ('The Man with the Golden Mousetrap', *The Daily Telegraph*, Nov 20).

Mr Saunders, as he then was, may perhaps have indulged in a little picturesque embroidery in his interview with Mr Spencer, who was not born at the time of which Saunders was speaking, the first night of *The Mousetrap* at the Theatre Royal, Nottingham over forty years ago.

As the original director of this once critically highly praised production of theatrical wonder, my recollection is still sharp enough to know that any alterations the author made could only have been effected with my consent and approval. There had of course been changes early on in rehearsal, which she agreed at my suggestion. Certainly Dame Agatha was far too professional in her work to favour any alterations that bypassed her director.

The play's reception in Nottingham was excellent and the local press generous; the first night paving the way for the successful tour and West End run that followed. These are *facts* – to dispute them now is to be more than economical with the truth.

How amusingly fanciful Sir Peter Saunders has become in his old age.

Appendix 8

First reviews of *The Mousetrap*

'There remain the alarming silences, which are perhaps the true test of such a piece upon the stage. That we feel them to be alarming can only be thanks to the producer, Mr Peter Cotes' – Anthony Cookman, *The Times*, 26 November 1952

'Directed with skill by Peter Cotes' – W.A. Darlington, *The Daily Telegraph*

'The play, tautly directed by Peter Cotes, has the expert merit of keeping us guessing to the very end' – Cecil Wilson, *Daily Mail*

'Even more thrilling than the plot is the atmosphere of shuddering suspense. . . .' – John Barber, *Daily Express*

'Peter Cotes, as producer, handles his company with discretion' – *The Stage*

'Peter Cotes proved, as a producer, that he is as much at home with Agatha as Ibsen' – Beverley Baxter, *Sunday Express*

'Peter Cotes's fast production never fluffs a thrill' – C.V. Cutis, *Show Business*

'. . . the brilliant direction of Peter Cotes' – Rossiter Shepherd, *The People*

'Mr Peter Cotes's production is taut and exciting' – Harold Hobson, *Sunday Times*

'The play is directed, with discreet understanding of the essentials, by Peter Cotes' – Kenneth Hurren, *What's On in London*

'Pleasantly acted and well produced (by Mr Peter Cotes)' – Peter Fleming, *The Spectator*

'The producer, Peter Cotes, has had great fun with his light, sound and heat' – *Western Sunday Independent*

'As the play proceeds, we realise that its manifold improbabilities have been calculated with anxious care. Peter Cotes has produced them skilfully' – J.C. Trewin, *The Lady*

'Mr Peter Cotes's direction is as discreet as a solicitor's letter' – Eric Keown, *Punch*

'The play is produced for every ounce of its tension by Mr Peter Cotes' – T.C. Worsley, *New Statesman & Nation*

'Mr Peter Cotes has produced so that all clues, true and false, are well displayed' – Frances Stephens, *Theatre World*

The Times
12 June 1985

Press Council rules against The Times

After reviving in a book review 12-year-old criticism of a theatrical producer, *The Times* should have published his letter replying to them, the Press Council said on Monday.

The Council upheld a complaint by Mr Peter Cotes that an article contained a significant inaccuracy which the newspaper declined to correct.

In a review of *Empty Seats*, the autobiography of producer Michael White, the reviewer, Irving Wardle, mentioned *The Mousetrap*, a book by another impresario, Peter Saunders. He said that in two sulphurously readable pages Mr Saunders settled accounts with Peter Cotes for his truncated rehearsals and vast subsequent earnings from the West End's longest runner.

Mr Cotes wrote in a letter for publication that one-sided versions of a dispute should never be accepted and published as fact unless thoroughly checked. The events described were fictitious and he had always denied them. He was not prepared for anyone to write from hearsay or secondhand a suggestion that he had lamentably failed in his obligations.

The deputy editor, Mr Colin Webb, replied that in the view of the arts editor there seemed no reason why Mr Wardle should not refer to material already published. Mr Wardle had simply said that accounts were settled in print with Mr Cotes.

Mr Cotes told the Press Coucil he had protested at lies and half-truths in *The Mousetrap Man* and that his rebuttals were included in another book, *The Mystery of Agatha Christie.*

At no time had it been agreed by him, or established by anyone else, that his rehearsals could properly be described as truncated or that there were vast subsequent earnings.

Mr Webb said a brief letter making those two points would certainly have been considered for publication, but that as nearly two months had then passed since publication it was really too late. He told the council that Mr Cotes' letter did not make clear what the substance of his complaint was.

The Press Council's adjudication was:

The Times's review of a new theatrical autobiography repeated serious criticism of a producer, Mr Peter Cotes, from a book published 12 years earlier. Mr Cotes had challenged the accuracy of its references to him years before. Having revived them by republication, the newspaper should have given him an opportunity to respond to them by publishing a letter.

The complaint against *The Times* is upheld.

Appendix 9

'and on . . . and on . . .'

In the wings

WHEN The Mousetrap goes into its 23rd year on Monday, it will be another landmark in the bank balance of Peter Cotes, who originally directed the play when it opened at the Ambassadors in 1952.

He is on a run-of-the-play percentage and, to date, the Agatha Christie thriller has been seen by more than 3,500,000 people and taken £2,750,000 at the box office.

However, not all of Mr Cotes's memories of his association with the production are happy ones, for he insisted on holding on to his percentage, despite the persuasions of impresario Peter Saunders to buy him out for a lump sum.

"I can say that I have made many thousands of pounds out of it," says Mr Cotes. "If I had sold out at the time I would have made less than a quarter. If you are one of the architects of success, you don't feel like sacrificing your interest. The artistic contribution is surely as great as the commercial."

Mr Cotes is writing a book about his associations with the play called The Origins of the Thriller, but he maintains: "The book will be written without any unpleasant resorting to personalities. If I did harbour any resentment at the time, I certainly don't now."

Likewise Mr Saunders, who says: "There was some disagreement at the time, but that is forgotten now. The offer I made was a generous one bearing in mind that the play was going through a bad time, although not so perhaps in retrospect."

Evening Standard
21 November 1974

Dame Agatha expected a six-month run

SIR—In Peterborough (Nov. 27) Sir Peter Saunders is quoted as saying that at the world premiere of The Mousetrap at the Theatre Royal, Nottingham, 35 years ago, the piece was "scheduled" for only three months. Not so. I prefer his earlier account of 1972, when he recalled the "betting" on the length of the run as being put at six months by the author herself and 14 months by the management.

Furthermore, your interview with Sir Peter suggests that it was a dispiriting first night. But as the director of that original production, first at Nottingham and subsequently at The Ambassadors in the West End, I must rebut any such suggestion.

I should also point out that Dame Agatha Christie was far too correct in her behaviour to "grab" pen or pencil and "re-write" (by cutting) before consulting with her director and leading players. To state otherwise does scant justice to a highly professional writer.
PETER COTES
London W1

The Daily Telegraph
3 Dec 1987

SUNDAY 29 NOVEMBER 1992

Talkback   Jeffrey Care

The sins of omission. Last week's Arts pages commemorated the fortieth anniversary of *The Mousetrap*, still playing before mystified audiences.

From a vintage Agatha Christie address, Hill Lawn Court, Chipping Norton, Oxfordshire, Peter Cotes wrote: 'I wondered, as the play's original director, why that fact went unacknowledged. The longest running little thriller (as Christie dubbed it) did, after all, have a director.'

The Observer
29 November 1992

Index